CFA Level 1. Study Notes for 2019

Financial Reporting and Analysis in one week

Preface

If you want to learn CFA easily and with less time, congratulations! You have the right book.

There are a couple of books available in the market which are good books, but in some areas, they create ambiguity. As a university lecturer for past ten years, I know how to make difficult concepts easy and understandable.

We started this book (it took almost a year to write this book) with the aim to provide cheapest but quality education and we will be providing more books like this in future.

We believe in simplicity and conciseness. This book is a complete and a comprehensive guide with simple language. This is our second updated version for CFA 2019.

You can learn the complete Financial Reporting & Analysis material in just one week with the help of this book and video lectures on video sharing websites like YouTube and daily motion.

We are open to suggestions and constructive critics.

Ok it's time to start reading and best of luck with your studies.

Regards

M. Imran Ahsan

Ch.imranahsen@gmail.com

Ch.imranahsen@skype

Ch.imranahsen (@youtube)

Table of contents

Introduction Study session 6

LOS21a: Describe the roles of financial reporting and financial statement analysis.

Financial reporting: These are the methods used by a firm/company to explain its financial position and financial health.

The management prepares unaudited and audited financial statements for the general public and the users of financial statements. The financial statements include income statements, balance sheet, statement of cash flow and other financial disclosures required by regulatory bodies/accounting standard setting bodies.

The users of financial statements are those who make economic decisions based on these reports like investors, Lenders, company management, Government, analysts, etc.

Financial statements analysis is about evaluating company`s performance by using these published financial reports. The information in the statements and in disclosures is used by analysts to evaluate company`s current and past performance to make an opinion about the firm like whether or not we should invest in this company. Or a bank can think of whether or not they should pass the loan application of this particular company.

LOS21b: Describe the roles of the statement of financial position, statement of comprehensive income, statement of changes in equity, and statement of cash flows in evaluating a company's performance and financial position.

Statements of Financial position: Statement of financial position is also called the balance sheet. It gives us information about company`s asset and liabilities and owner`s equity at some particular date.

The balance sheet is very useful as it gives us the information about resources owned by the company (assets) and how the company has financed those resources (liabilities and shareholder`s equity). Analysts use this information to evaluate the company.

Assets – liabilities = residual claim in company by owners.

Statement of comprehensive income: Statement of comprehensive income shows all changes in equity except for shareholder`s transactions. Depending on local regulations, it may be combines into two parts (or reported separately)
- The income statement.
- The statement of other comprehensive income.

The income statement: It shows the revenues and expenses from ordinary business operations.
Revenues are inflows by selling goods and or services from normal business activities.
Expenses are outflows (from purchasing raw material and services etc.) from producing those goods and services.

Other comprehensive income: It generally shows the revenues and expenses from the unusual events and from the items which do not come into normal course of business operations like actuarial gains/losses due to foreign exchange rate changes etc.

Statement of changes in equity: We know that; Assets – liabilities = shareholder`s equity. It is the total residual claims of owners into company.
Changes in shareholder`s equity is the statements which shows how the value of shareholder`s (owner`s) has changed over time.
There are three components of equity
Paid in capital: The money received by the company by selling its shares.
Retained earnings: These are the undistributed profits.
Treasury stock: Sometimes companies buy their own stock. It is the total amount given to investors for buying the stock.

Statement of cash flows: One of the most important document a company have. It shows the cash receipts and payments of company. These cash flows are grouped into three categories;
CFO, Cash flow from operations: The cash inflows and out flows from main business/normal business activities came under this category.
CFI, Cash flow from investing activities: Cash received or paid from the activities like sale/acquisition of fixed asset (property, plant and equipment etc.) or investments in other firms etc.
CFF, Cash flow from financing activities: Cash inflows/outflows from issuing/ retiring of debt or equity securities. It also includes payment of dividends.
Note: We will discuss in detail all above concepts. Purpose of this section is only to have some overview.

LOS21c: Describe the importance of financial statement notes and supplementary information including disclosures of accounting policies, methods and estimates and management's commentary.

There are two major company`s financial disclosures
- Footnotes
- The management's discussion and analysis.

The footnotes: The footnotes to the financial statements help us to understand company`s position and performance. They give us information about company`s fiscal year, standards used in preparation of financial statements, accounting assumptions, insight about unique transactions and about legal proceedings, employee`s benefit plans, contingencies and commitments, acquisitions and disposals of businesses and segments of the firm. (We will discuss all of these later).

Management`s commentary: Also known as the management's discussion and analysis (MD&A), management's report, operating and financial review.

This is also a very crucial source of information for an analyst to understand financial reports. One thing to remember here, the MD&A is generally unaudited.

IFRS guidelines suggests to have following information in this section,

Nature of the business, objectives of management, company's past performance, current business environment and future outlook, the performance measures used, the company's important relationships, resources owned by the company, and risks.

US GAAP requires that MD&A must include
- Major Events and future uncertainties which will affect liquidity, capital resources and main operations of the firm.
- Inflation and off-balance sheet items, obligations like purchase /sale agreements or any other contractual agreement.
- Accounting policies based on management`s judgment.

LOS21d: Describe the objective of audits of financial statements the types of audit reports and the importance of effective internal controls.

Audit: An audit is inspection of financial statements and supporting documents by independent body (an auditor or body of auditors).

Objective of audit: The objective of audit is to create an opinion about the fairness and reliability of a set of financial statements and documents.

The independent auditor(s) is employed by a board of directors of a company. The auditor is to check whether or not accounting standards has been followed. They also check the company`s internal control system, confirms assets and liabilities and determine, is there any material error exists in the financial statements.

The auditor`s examination produces auditor`s report which has three parts.

- A statement that the auditor has performed an independent review.
- A statement that generally accepted auditing standards were followed and there is a reasonable assurance that the financial documents have no material error.
- A statement that the auditor is satisfied about the chosen and following accounting standard. Reasonable estimates and assumption along with proper accounting policies were chosen.

Types of report: Auditor`s opinion can be one of the following three (also called three types of report)

Unqualified opinion/report: This is the most common type of report. It is also called clean report. It suggests that (according to the auditor`s view) the financial documents are free of any material errors or omissions and financial statements has been prepared by following the accounting standards.

Qualified opinion/report: It suggests that some exceptions have made to the accounting principles in preparation of financial statements. The auditor explains these exceptions in his report.

Adverse opinion: If auditor found faults in financial statements like the statements do not conform with accounting principles or financial statements are not presented fairly, he issues adverse opinion/report. Adverse opinion is also issued in case If auditor is unable to give an opinion due to limited scope or non-availability of proper documents. Adverse report tells us these reports are not reliable at all.

Effective internal controls.

Internal control is the process by which firm tries to ensure the fair and accurate presentation of its financial statements.

Internal control is the responsibility of management. They should keep checking the balances so the auditor can validate them. In USA for the public traded company the auditor must express his/her opinion about internal control with or separate to auditor`s report.

LOS21e: Identify and describe information sources that analysts use in financial statement analysis besides annual financial statements and supplementary information.

We know that the companies are required to issue annual reports to show their financial results and performances. But in meantime companies also releases quarterly and semi annually reports which analyst must consider while evaluating the performance of the company. These interim reports (generally un audited) and their footnotes are a vital source of information to an analyst. Because these statements show major financial events during that interim.

Other important sources of information are Securities and Exchange commission filings like,

Form 8-K: Under form 8 K the companies are required to disclose

- Acquisitions and disposals of major assets
- Changes in management or corporate governance.

This is form is submitted when changes occur so this is very important one.

Quarterly financial statements are filed under **Form 10-Q.** This also include any material changes in business and any new information regarding company`s management.

Form 10-k: It is filed with audited **annual reports,** information about the business, management and legal matters.

Proxy statements: when there are matters which require shareholder`s votes this statement is issued to them. The matters like election of board of directors, their compensation etc.

Sources of information other than SEC filings;

Press releases and corporate reports: Companies often releases these items. They can be a source of information up to some extent.

Conference calls: This is another important source for an analyst. After earnings are announced senor management answer the questions in conference call.

Earnings guidance is given by the management to presents its own performance expectations.

Industry reports: the reports of industry and especially the competitors are also good source of information.

Analyst must also consider economic conditions of businesses and country in analyzing the companies. He/she can get more information from economic and business journals, statistical journals and govt. journals.

LOS21f: Describe the steps in the financial statement analysis framework.

Following is a six-step basic framework for any of above motivation also called six steps in the financial analysis framework.

1. Articulate the purpose and the context of the analysis
2. Collect data
3. Process the data
4. Analyze and interpret the data
5. Develop reports and communicate the conclusions
6. Follow up/update the analysis

1. **Articulate the purpose and the context of the analysis:** First of all, we need to articulate what is the purpose of our analysis. An analyst might be working on different perspectives to evaluate a company. These perspectives might include

Evaluation of a company as an equity investment, Potential acquisition, analysis about company`s credit worthiness or any other intentions given by client.

2. **Collect data:** At this stage all the sources of information like financial statements, management`s commentary, conference calls etc. are needed to collect the data about a company.

3. **Process the data:** At this stage all the data collected in previous stage is processed. We might be calculating financial ratios and common size statements, building models or forecasting etc.

4. **Analyze and interpret the data:** At this stage we start to build an assessment about the company. We answer the questions we were looking for in first stage.

5. **Develop reports and communicate the conclusions:** At this stage we draw conclusions and develop a report and communicate it with intended audience/client. Report must comply with Codes and Standards.

6. **Follow up/update the analysis:** At this stage we gather and update our previously collected data/information and update our conclusions. Updating might include repetition of some previous steps.

Financial Reporting Standards   Study session 6

LOS 22 a: Describe the objective of the financial statements and the importance of financial reporting standards in security analysis and valuation.

Objective of financial statements

According to the IASB Conceptual Framework for Financial Reporting 2010, the objective of financial statements is to provide useful information about the company to current and potential Investors, Creditors and Lenders to help them in decision making about lending or investment in the company.

Importance

These standards ensure

Consistency: it means that these statements should be using consistent methods of calculations and presentation. Similar items must be treated in similar way.

Comparability: The financial statements should be comparable. Although they are not hundred percent same but they should be in format which helps comparison.

LOS 22b: Describe roles and desirable attributes of financial reporting standards-setting bodies and regulatory authorities in establishing and enforcing reporting standards, and describe the role of international organizations of securities commissions

Standard setting bodies set the financial reporting standards Regulatory bodies enforce them.

Standard setting bodies:

These are independent not for profit organizations. These bodies consist of professional accountants and auditors. There are two major standard setting bodies, FASB (federal accounting standard board) in US which established US GAAP (Generally accepted accounting principles).

IASB (International Accounting standard board) which set forth IFRS (international financial reporting standards) for rest of the world.

Many countries have their own standard setting bodies too. FASB and other bodies are working towards convergence with IFRS.

Desirable qualities and attribute of these bodies.

- Sufficient resources, capability and authority

- Clear and consistent standard setting process
- Independent, but connected to the stakeholders.
- Driven to act in the general public interest. (not self-interest)

Regulatory authorities:

Regulatory authorities enforce the standards set by standard setting bodies. SEC (Securities and Exchange Commission in US and FCA (financial conduct authority) in UK are some examples.

Most of these work for IOSCO (International organization of securities commission). It is an organization to guide those who regulate local markets. Its members regulate 90 percent of the financial markets.

IOSCO has three objectives 1.Protect investor   2.Ensure the market is efficient, fair and transparent   3.   Reduced systematic risk

Following are some fillings for public limited companies, required by SEC (Securities and Exchange Commission, a regulatory authority). These are very importance source of information for an analyst.

Form S-1 Registration statement: It is filed prior to the issuance of new security.It contains details about issuer, the underwriter, the risk associated with security and disclosure about the usage of funds.

10-K annual filing: It is an annual filing, contains statement about business and audited financial statements. It also contains legal matters about the company. Equivalent to 10-k SEC forms for foreign issuers in the U.S. markets are Form 40-F and Form 20-F for Canadian companies and other foreign issuers respectively.

10Q Quarterly filing: It is filed quarterly. It contains any material changes in business and unaudited updates to the financial statements.

DEF-14 A Proxy statement: It is a statement to SEC which contains the matters about shareholder`s votes.

8K major material event: This form contains major changes in assets acquisition or disposal. Changes in corporate governance and or management or any other accounting policy changes. it is filed whenever the changes occur. So, its very important for an analyst.

144 Issuance of qualified buyers: In some cases, a company may issue securities to a group of qualified buyers. Company may not have to register security with SEC but they are still required to notify SEC with form 144 about this intention.

Forms 3, 4, and 5: These contain beneficial ownership of securities by a company's directors and officers. Analyst can get information from these forms to know about purchases and sales of securities inside the company.

LOS 22C: Describe the status of global convergence of accounting standards and ongoing barriers to developing one universally accepted set of financial reporting standards.

Status of global convergence: Reasonable efforts have made to comply with IFRS. In Europe companies are needed to comply with IFRS. In US if a company comply with IFRS the SEC do not enforce it to comply with US GAAP. Globally regulatory authorities are making efforts to come align with IFRS.

Ongoing barriers:

- The standards setting bodies and regulatory authorities do disagree on certain item`s treatment.
- There is much cost involved while changes in standards and their implications on existing standards.
- There is much political pressure from business cartels/business groups on local regulatory authorities if they change the standards.

LOS 22 d: Describe the International Accounting Standards Board's conceptual framework, including the objective and qualitative characteristics of financial statements, required reporting elements, and constraints and assumptions in preparing financial statements.

The objective of the IASB framework is to provide useful financial information to those who are providing resource to the company (i.e. investor, creditors)

The framework outlines the qualitative characteristics, specifies required financial statement elements and provides various assumptions and constraints in preparation of financial reports to make financial statements useful.

Qualitative characteristics

There are two basic qualitative characteristics that make financial statements useful.

1. Relevance: Information is relative if it is predictive and confirmatory. It means information in financial statements must help the user (with reasonable accounting/financial knowledge) to predict the future and confirm the current state of the company. It also means materiality of information.

2. Faithful presentation: It means the information is complete, neutral and free of error.

Frame work also provides us four more characteristics which ensure relevance and faithful presentation.

i. **Comparability:** It means the financial statements must be in a format so they can be easily comparable. The presentation must be consistent among entities and periods.

ii.   **Verifiability:** It means that the experts should be able to get the same information by using same methods.

iii.   **Timeliness:** it means the information is provided before decision maker need to make decisions.

iv.   **Understandability:** it means that those who has reasonable understanding of the accounting and those who have made reasonable effort should be able to understand that information.

Required reporting elements

The framework provides us five groups of required reporting elements. From which three groups measures financial position while two measures financial performance.

Financial position measuring elements are:

- Assets: The resources owned by the company.
- Liabilities: The obligations of a company.
- Equity: The residual interest of owners in company. This is what left after deducting the liabilities from assets.

Financial performance elements are:

- Incomes: Inflows from the normal business or gains from extraordinary events (not from owner`s contribution).
- Expenses: Outflows from normal course of business and losses from extraordinary events.

Recognition and measurement of the elements in the accounts

Recognition*:* it means that an item need to be recognized if it has probable inflow or outflow and it`s cost could be reliably measured.

Measurement*:* The amount at which the elements are reported depends upon the measurement base. There are six possibilities which can be used to measure the value.

i.   Historical cost: The amount originally paid to purchase an asset.

ii.   Amortized cost: Historical cost minus accumulated depreciation.

iii.   Current cost: The amount that that can be used to buy an equivalent asset at today's market value.

iv.   Settlement value: It means the amount an asset could be sold for or the amount needed to satisfy a liability.

v.   Present value: A discounted value of future expected cash flows from that item.

vi.   Fair value: The amount that would be exchanged between knowledgeable parties in an arm's length transaction (easily and quickly).

Constraints and assumptions for the preparation of financial statements.

Constraints: The framework provides us two major constraints in preparation of financial statements so they can be useful.

i. Cost vs Benefit: The cost of presenting information should be less than the benefits gained from using it.

ii. Non-quantifiable information: There are some important information which are highly important for the company`s future profitability but they could not be presented in financial statements because they are not quantifiable. For example, customer loyalty, employee loyalty, environment. They must be considered in company analysis.

Assumptions: There are two assumptions that framework provides us

Accrual accounting: It means that the economic transaction must be presented in a period in which they occur not necessarily with cash payment.

i. Going concern: It means the company is expected to continue in existence for the foreseeable future. As we can imagine that we may have entirely different opinion about value of company if it is going to close next year.

ii.

LOS 22e: Describe general requirements of financial statements under international financial reporting standards (IFRS).

IAS1 (International Accounting Standard 1) tells us which financial statements are required and how they must be presented.

Required statements:

If a company want to comply with IAS1 they must provide Balance sheet, Statement of comprehensive income, Cash flow statement, Statement of owner`s equity and set of notes (contains explanation of the accounting policies and significant events necessary to fully understand the statements).

General features:

According to IAS 1 financial statements must have following features

a. **Fair presentation:** The statements must present the transactions or events faithfully by following the criteria set out in the framework.
b. **Going concern:** the IAS 1 tells us to present the financial statement with an assumption of going concern (that the company is not going to be liquidated in near future).
c. **Accrual accounting:** The accrual accounting principle must be followed in preparation of financial statements.
d. **Consistency:** The information presented should be consistent between periods. The items should not change significantly from period to period without a significant change in business.
e. **Materiality:** It means that the item that could influence a decision using these statements must not be omitted.
f. **Aggregation**: Similar items should be presented together and dissimilar items must be reported separately.
g. **No offsetting**: The statements must clearly present assets and liabilities as well as income and expenditures in full. If not specifically guided by IFRS they must not be offset.
h. **Frequency:** Financial statements must be released at least annually.

i.   **Comparative information:** Information from prior period must be provided along with the current material so they can be compared.

Required structure/ contents:

There are three distinct required contents.

Balance sheet must be classified as current and not current items (assets and liabilities).

There are some elements the IFRS requires minimum information about them, must be included. For example, balance sheet must show specific items such as cash and cash equivalents, plant, property and equipment, and inventories. In the comprehensive income statement revenues, profit or loss, tax expense, and finance costs among others must be included.

The statements must provide comparative information for all items from prior periods unless there is another IAS rule with contradict to this rule.

LOS 22f: compare the key concepts of financial reporting standards under IFRS and US generally accepted accounting principles (US GAAP) reporting systems.

US GAAP and IFRS differs in form of Performance elements, recognition of assets, upward valuation of assets.

The performance elements:

IFSR has only two elements listed as performance elements   Income Expenses

IFRS defines assets as <u>resource from which future economic benefit is expected.</u>

US GAAP has four performance elements   Revenues   Expenses   Gains and losses   Comprehensive income

Under GAAP Assets are defined as future economic benefits.

The measurements and evaluation are the same in both. The IFRS allows upward valuation of assets but GAAP does not allow in case of most of the assets. GAAP allows the upward evaluation in case of some assets which are needed to be held at fair value.

Note: Upward valuation will be discussed later in this book in detail

LOS 22g: Identify characteristics of a coherent financial reporting framework and the barriers to creating such a framework.

A coherent framework must fulfill following three characteristics;

1.   **Transparency:** The statements must reflect the underlying business activity more clearly (fair and full disclosure).

2.   **Comprehensiveness:** No important transaction should be omitted. The statements must completely cover all the financial transactions affecting business.

3.   **Consistency:** Similar transaction must be treated in similar way allowing comparison across industries and periods.

Barriers to creating coherent financial reporting framework
There are some conflicts exist at certain areas in achieving these characteristics called **barriers** which are,
1.Valuation: There are various methods to value assets and liabilities. For example, historical cost, amortized cost etc. Sometime we need subjective judgment to use appropriate method. And many time choices of methods changed from firm to firm.

2.Standard setting: US GAAP is known as rules-based approach to standard setting, where the IFRS is known as principle-based approach. Different parties with different agendas have different and opposing opinions on validity of these approaches.
3.Measurement: The balance sheet and income statement are inter related. But the balance sheet is reported at a single point of time while the income statement is presented as performance over a period of time. The standard setters mostly set preference on focusing on balance sheet. Other may rely more on income/ expense approach (i.e. Income statement).

LOS 22 h: Describe implications for financial analysis of differing financial reporting systems and the importance of monitoring developments in financial reporting standards.

As the Accounting standards are continuously evolving, an analyst must remain updated about these changes and innovations. Analyst must visit professional journals, IASB website (*www.ifrs.org*)andFASB website(*www.fasb.org*). CFA institute also issues position papers on financial reporting issues.
Analyst must also check for company`s disclosures for accounting standards used, accounting policies and estimates.

LOS 22 i: Analyze company disclosures of significant accounting policies.

Accounting assumptions and policies used by company must be disclosed in footnotes of the financial statements. Anything regarding the subjective management decisions must be reported in Management discussion& analysis.
There are two types of accounting policies disclosures.
1.   **Accounting policies disclosure:** These disclosures are a source of extra information about contents of financial statements.

2. **Changes to accounting policies:** This disclosure is also a vital source of information. This helps us to judge the management team itself and the expected outcomes of these changes in future.

Understanding Income Statement   Study session 7

LOS 23 a: Describe the components of the income statement and alternative presentation formats of that statement.

The income statement is known under many names like
- The income statement.
- The statement of operations.
- The statement of earnings.
- The profit and loss statement.

Whatever the name is, it tells us about revenues and costs of the company in one financial year.

Components of the income statement.

We know that
Net income =Revenue - expenses
Revenue is the company's income from the normal course of business i.e from their everyday activities.
Net revenue is revenue that has been adjusted for discounts or potential returns. (discount on sales or sales returns)
Expenses The costs incurred while generating revenues. We have cost of raw material, labor cost, rent etc.
Gains and losses: The incomes and costs which are not associated with ordinary business activities. For example, if a company sells its plant and get some Gain (profit) or loss.

Revenues + other sources of income + extraordinary gains - ordinary business expenses - other expenses - extra ordinary losses = **net income**

Alternative presentations.

Different companies present income statement items differently

For example, some companies put current year items on left and others on right.

Some companies use brackets or parentheses when reporting an item that reduces income (i.e. expenses). Other companies use negative sign. Companies often choose to aggregate certain items together on the report. Selling general and administration expenses for example, some companies report this as a single line item while others report them separately.

Companies aggregate the items according to following

Grouping by nature: Grouping by nature means anything that is basically the same should be listed on the one line for example and all kinds of depreciation (depreciation of all long-term assets) would all be grouped together as one item on the report.

Grouping by function: In this method, revenues or expenses are grouped as they have certain link. For example, in cost of goods sold we have bunch of different expenses which are related to the cost of sold goods (i.e. raw material, labor wages, etc.)

Single step VS multistep presentation

This is another difference in presentation of income statement. In single step format companies put all revenues together and all expenses together. They do not report gross profit or gross loss. Gross profit or losses are presented in multi-step format.

LOS 23b: Describe general principles of revenue recognition and accrual accounting, specific revenue recognition applications (including accounting for long-term contracts, installment sales, barter transactions, gross and net reporting of revenue), and implications of revenue recognition principles for financial analysis.

Remember revenues do not depend upon cash. When goods are sold on credit revenue is recognized when
• Ownership of the goods changes hands from selling to buying party.
• When the risk and reward of owning goods has moved to a buying party.

With IFRS we must recognize revenues in sale of goods under following conditions.
• When the risk and reward of owning goods has moved to a buying party.
• Selling party has no managerial influence/control over the goods.

- The expected revenue can be reliably measured.
- It is likely and probable that economic benefit of the transaction will flow to the selling entity.
- The cost of the transaction can be reliably measures.

In case of the delivery of services following conditions are followed
- The expected revenue can be reliably measured.
- It is likely and probable that the economic benefits of transactions will flow to the selling party.
- Cost of the transaction can be measured.
- Stage of the completion of the transaction must be reliably measured.

With GAAP, revenue must be recognized if it is
Realized, realizable or earned.

These are some special cases in which revenue recognition becomes more difficult.
Special cases can be
- long term contracts
- Installment sales.
- Barter transactions.
- The gross and net reporting of revenue.

Long term contracts: Long term contracts mean revenue streams will cover multiple accounting periods (more than one year).

The issue is when do we recognize the revenue? If we recognize it when the contract occurred, that will exaggerate reported income in the current period and the income for subsequent years will be underweight.

So, we need to divide the overall revenue amount across multiple years maybe an equal are prorated(unequal) distribution across each year or maybe recognition should be based on our understanding of the underlying business circumstances using a method called

i. *Percentage of completion.*

It estimates what percentage of the contract is complete. If the contract is 60 % complete then 60 % of the revenue should be recognized by the company up to that point. We calculate the percentage of completion of a project by calculating, what percentage of total cost we have spent.

For example, a company has entered into a project which will take five years to complete.

Total cost of the project is estimated = $20 million
Price at which it will be sold =$30 m.
In the first year, we spend 5million which is 25 percent of the overall cost.

So, the 25% of total revenues (25% of 30 m) should be reported for first year and same method for next years.

ii. *If the outcome of the project is not actually known at the beginning (of long term contract).*

IFRS and U. S. GAAP differ in this circumstance.

Under IFRS as long as we have sufficient incoming revenue to justify the level of spending we can recognize revenue to the extent of the costs incurred. It means, revenues =costs. Profit is only recognized at completion.

Under US GAAP we use completed contract method. The project doesn't go to the income statement at all. Only loss is recognized immediately. The cumulative cost a recorded on the balance sheet where cash is going down as it is spent. And some other asset (inventory) is rising as the project is in his way to completed. In final year we record total revenue and total cost. In years other than final we do not recognize any cost or revenues under US GAAP.

Installment sales (Another long-term contract)
This is a situation where sales proceeds are to be received in installments over multiple periods.

Under IFRS the expected installment payments are discounted back to their present value. That discounted amount is then recognized on the date of the sale as the sales price. The remainder, the difference between the simple sum of payments and the present value of those payments will be recognized over time as an interest component.

Under U.S GAAP we have two methods
• Installment method
• Cost recovery method
Let's understand these two with the help of an example.
Let's say a company is selling one of their plant.

The cost of the plant was $5m and they have agreed a price of $8m. The buying party has offered a down payment of $1.5m and remaining $6.5 m will be paid over a period of 10 years.

Under the installment method a portion of profit is recognized in line with the percentage of the total sales price which is profit.

In our case the total profit is $3 m which is 37.5 % of total deal value ($8m)

Then we take 37.5 % of the down payment (1.5 m) to get a profit attributable to the down payment of $562500.

And whenever we receive cash its 37.5 percent will be recognized as profit and remaining is cost.

Cost recovery method: In this method profit cannot be recorded until the amount of cash is greater than the initial cost so because the cash amount paid by the buyer is not higher than the original cost no profit would be recorded unless when the cash amount supersedes the cost it will be recorded as profit in coming periods.

Barter transactions:
Let's say two companies exchanging advertising space. It means they are exchanging very similar assets or services to each other.

So, there should be very little or no effect on income.

Under IFRS revenue can be recognized from this type of transaction in an amount equal to that from a similar non-barter transaction between unrelated parties.

Under US GAAP we can only recognized revenue from barter transaction if we have previously recognized cash for a similar transaction.

LOS 23c: Calculate revenue given information that might influence the choice of revenue recognition method.

Normally firms buy products and or raw materials from their suppliers and sell to their customers. So, cost of goods sold and revenues are easily distinguishable.

With E. business companies were selling products that they never purchased or manufactured. They simply take in the revenue and then arrange delivery to the customer directly from the supplier.

The question is should they be reporting revenue in the full amount received from the customer (called gross revenue reporting) or their earnings only (called net revenues reporting) since earnings are more like a commission as the spread between the amount they have received in the cost of them from the supplier.

Under U. S. GAAP: If the following conditions are fulfilled the firm can report gross revenues otherwise net revenues.
- If selling company is the primary under a contract.
- If they bear inventory risk and credit risk.
- If they have more than one supplier.

- They have reasonable influence over the price.

LOS 23.d: Describe key aspects of the converged accounting standards for revenue recognition issued by the International Accounting Standards Board and Financial Accounting Standards Board in May 2014.

In May 2014, the IASB and FASB issued converged accounting standards so a principles-based approach can be provided for revenues recognition. The pivotal principle behind these converged standards is that revenue must be recognized when the goods and or services has been transferred to the customers. This is the principle already known as "the revenues must be recognized when earned.

Revenue Recognition Steps

There are five steps involved in recognizing revenue:

1. Identify the contract (or contracts) pertaining to a customer
2. Identify performance obligations in the contract
3. Determine the transaction price (or prices)
4. Allocate the transaction price (or prices) to the performance obligations in each contract
5. Recognize revenue whenever the entity satisfies a performance obligation.

Key Aspects of the Converged Accounting Standards

Following are the key aspects of the converged accounting standard for revenue recognition issued by the IASB in May 2014

• A contract is an agreement and commitment between two or more parties which establishes each party's obligations and rights, including payment terms, and which exists only if collectability is probable. Under US GAAP, "probable" means "likely to occur", while under IFRS, it means "more likely than not".

• Performance obligations within contracts represent promises to transfer distinct goods or services. A good or service is considered to be "distinct" if the customer can benefit from it on its own or in combination with readily available resources and if the promise to transfer it can be separated from other promises in the contract. Each performance obligation that is identified is to be accounted for separately.

• The transaction price is the seller's estimate of the amount that will be received in exchange for the transfer of goods or services identified in the contract and are allocated to each identified performance obligation.

•   Revenue will be recognized whenever a performance obligation is fulfilled. Once revenue is recognized, a contract asset is presented on the balance sheet.

•   A receivable will appear on the seller's balance sheet when all performance obligations have been met except for payment. A contract liability will be presented on the balance sheet if consideration is received in advance of transferring goods or services.

•   The incremental costs for obtaining a contract and other costs incurred to fulfill a contract must be capitalized or reported as an asset on the balance sheet rather than as an expense on the income statement. The profitability of companies which had previously expensed these incremental costs in the years prior to adopting the converged standard will initially appear to be higher under the converged standards.

At the end of a financial year, companies are required to disclose information about their contracts with customers classified into different categories of contracts. These categories can be based on the type of product, the geographic region, the type of customer or sales channel, the type of contract pricing terms, the contract duration, or the timing of transfers. Companies must also disclose the balances of any contract-related assets and liabilities and significant changes in those balances, as well as remaining performance obligations and transaction price allocated to those obligations, and any significant judgments and changes in judgments that are related to revenue recognition. Significant judgments are those used in determining the timing and amounts of revenue to be recognized.

LOS 23.e: Describe general principles of expense recognition, specific expense recognition applications, and implications of expense recognition choices for financial analysis.

Expenses: The IASB Conceptual Framework describes expenses as "decreases in economic benefits during the accounting period in the form of outflows or depletions of assets or increase in liabilities that result in decreases in equity, other than those relating to distributions to equity participants."

General Principles of Expense Recognition: A company recognizes expenses in the period that it consumes the economic benefits associated with the expenditure or loses some previously recognized economic benefit.

Matching principle: Under the matching principle, a company recognizes some expenses (for example, cost of goods sold) whenever the associated revenues are recognized. Matching requires that a company recognizes the cost of goods sold in the same period as revenues from the sale of the goods. **Matching applied to inventory and cost of goods sold**.

Period costs are expenditures which less directly match revenue and are reflected in the period when a company has the expenditure or incurs a liability. For example, administrative expenses.

Specific identification method, the inventory and cost of goods sold are based on their physical flow. IFRS and US GAAP, however, permit the use of the first in, first out (FIFO) method, and the weighted average cost method to assign costs.

FIFO method: In this method oldest goods that are purchased/manufactured are sold first while the newest goods purchased or manufactured remain in inventory. So, the ending inventory would include the most recent purchases.

Weighted average cost method: In this method the average costs of goods available for sale are assigned to the units sold and the units remaining in inventory.

Last in, first out (LIFO) method: This method is only allowed under US GAAP, but IFRS does not permit it. Under this method the newest goods that are purchased/manufactured are sold first while the oldest goods purchased/manufactured remained in inventory. So, the costs of the newest items purchased will flow into the costs of goods sold first.

Specific Expense Recognition Applications

Doubtful accounts: While using matching principle, once revenue is recognized, a company is required to record an estimate of uncollectible revenues. This estimate is recorded as uncollectable reserve/ reserve for doubtable debts (an expense) on the income statement, not deducted from revenues directly.

Warranties: While recognizing revenues from sales of warrantable goods and or services, companies are required to estimate the amount of future expenses which might result from these warranties, to recognize estimated warranty expenses in the periods of sale (not in a later date).

Depreciation and Amortization: Depreciation is the process of systematically allocating the costs of long-lived assets over their useful life. There are many methods for computing depreciation. These are straight-line method, diminishing balance method and the units of production method.

Straight-line method: Under this method cost of long-lived assets less the estimated residual value is allocated evenly over the estimated useful life of the asset.

Annual Depreciation under straight line method = $\dfrac{Cost - residual\ value}{Useful\ life}$

Example: ABS company purchases machinery at cost of $10 m. they expect to use it for 10 years after which they will sell it for $1m. Calculate annual depreciation using straight lie method.

Solution: We know the formula for straight lie method, Annual Depreciation under straight line method = $\dfrac{Cost - residual\ value}{Useful\ life}$

By putting values in our formula, we got, annual depreciation = $\dfrac{10m - 1m}{10}$ =900000$

Diminishing balance method and the units of production methods are referred to as **accelerated methods of depreciation** because they accelerate the timing of depreciation by allocating a greater proportion of the depreciation expense to the early years of an asset's useful life.

Amortization Expense Recognition
The term amortization is used whenever the long-lived assets are intangible and have a finite, useful life. Amortization expense should match the proportion of the asset's benefits used during the period. Many firms use the straight-line method to calculate annual amortization expense. Straight-line amortization is exactly like straight-line depreciation. Intangible assets who have indefinite lives like goodwill are not amortized must be tested for impairment at least annually. If the asset value is impaired, an expense equal to the impairment amount is recognized on the income statement.

Implications of Expense Recognition Choices for Financial Analysis
The choice of depreciation or amortization method, as well as the estimate of useful life and residual value, can affect a company's reported net income. Also, the estimates that the company uses for doubtful debts and warranty expenses affect net income.

An analyst, having familiarities with the monetary effects of different expense recognition policies and estimates, can efficiently compare different companies or within a single company's historical performance. These effects may be used to adjust for better comparison.

LOS 23f: Describe the financial reporting treatment and analysis of non-recurring items (including discontinued operations, unusual or infrequent items) and changes in accounting standards.

When evaluating a company's future earnings, it important to separate incomes and expenses that are likely to continue in the future from those that are less likely to continue.

IFRS and U. S. GAAP do offer some guidelines to separate them but some items have less clear future and requires some judgment from analyst. *We are going to look in*
1. Discontinued operations
2. Extraordinary items.
3. Unusual or infrequent items.
4. Changes in accounting policies
5. Operating versus non-operating items.

A discontinued operation is a part of the business which is being disposed of. It means that part is not going to play any role in future.

Both US GAAP and IFRS require this to report on the income statement separately as a discontinued operation. Since that part of the business will not drive revenue in future, it is eliminated when developing a forecast.

Extraordinary Items: Items of income and expense that are considered both infrequent and unusual are considered extraordinary.

This classification is not permitted under IFRS. After December 2015, US GAAP also does not permit this classification. But before December 2015 under U. S. GAAP this classification existed.

Unusual or infrequent items: These are reported before tax with continued operations.

Items that are considered in this category includes
- Sale of the business unit at a considerable premium (gains) or discount (losses).
- Gains or losses from Impairments, write-offs, write-downs, restructuring charges.

Under US GAAP items which are either unusual or infrequent are not considered extraordinary you need to be both unusual and infrequent for that classification.

For example, restructuring charges or the sale of the business unit at a considerable premium or discount. These items will be reported with the company's continuing operations.

Under IFRS the accounting treatment is a bit different. Based on the idea that a single income or expense that is material or relevant to the understanding of the business should be reported separately anything unusual or infrequent would have to be reported separately.

Changes in accounting policies:

The change in accounting policy could be of two types.

- A new accounting standard set up by the standard setting authority or company decided to move from IFRS to GAAP or other way around.
- Changes in accounting estimates

Changes in applicable accounting standards are required to be applied retrospectively. It means whenever a company changes its accounting standard, they are required to restate their previous financial statements according to new standards because it would be misleading for a company to be able to use two different sets of accounting standards on the same document side by side. (Use of LIFO is an exception here. We will discuss it under inventories in detail)

Change in an accounting estimate: The effect of a change in an accounting estimate is not required to be applied retrospectively. Because it depends upon the management`s judgment usually after getting new information.

For example, if the management realizes that some specific asset has longer or shorter useful life than previously estimated. It will significantly change expense (depreciation) and it required to be mentioned in the notes accompanying the statement.

Analytical implications:

In forecasting there is considerable judgment in the end of analyst is needed. The analyst has to decide whether he should include any item or remove it from analysis. Analyst must see whether or not new policies have their effects on cash flow. If they have, the more care is required at the end of analyst to include or exclude items from the analysis. Changes in standards are disclosed and the documents are restated according to new standards, so there is not much to worry in this case.

LOS 23g: Distinguish between the operating and non-operating components of the income statement.

Operating and Non-operating items.

First of all, we need to understand the <u>central business activities of the</u> <u>company</u>.

If a company delivers a specific good and or service, all revenues and costs associated with those goods and or services are considered operating items. <u>Any revenue or cost not associated with company's central business is more</u> <u>than likely a non-operating item and must be reported separately.</u>
For example, a non-financial services company's interest on debt and dividends on equity would be more likely non-operating items
On the other hand, financial services company must classify interest and or dividends as operating items.
<u>*So, the activities related to core business are operating while other*</u> <u>*activities are called non-operating activities.*</u>

Both IFRS and U. S. GAAP have some specific rules on interest and dividends and where they should be reported in certain circumstances. But as an analyst the main goal is to understand the reasoning a company has for holding an investment.

LOS 23h: Describe how earnings per share is calculated and calculate and interpret a company's earnings per share (both basic and diluted earnings per share) for both simple and complex capital structures.

LOS 23i: Distinguish between dilutive and anti-dilutive securities and described the implications of each for the earnings per share calculation.

Simple and complex capital structure: If a company issues any financial instruments that can be converted into common stock then we have a complex capital structure, and if not, it means we have simple capital structure.

EPS stands for earnings per share and basic EPS is just that. Basic EPS = company's earnings that are available for distribution to common stockholders / weighted average number of shares of common stock outstanding

Diluted EPS takes a company's complex capital structure into account.

<u>Basic and diluted the EPS are the same if the company has a simple capital</u> <u>structure.</u>
Diluted EPS is a performance metric used to gauge the quality of a company's **earnings per share** (**EPS**) if all convertible securities were exercised (converted

into common stock). If convertibles exist, they bring down the diluted EPS down from basic EPS.

Dilutive and anti-dilutive securities:
Dilutive securities are those that bring up the number of shares outstanding in the calculation of diluted EPS and bring the EPS figure down.
Anti-dilutive securities are those that if they were converted and included would bring EPS up.

LOS 23 j: Convert income statements to common size income statements
LOS 23 k: Evaluate a company's financial performance using common size income statements and financial ratios based on the income statement.

Common size analysis of the income statement:
When building a vertical common size income statement, every item in income statement is described in terms of as a percentage of revenue. (i.e. $\frac{Cost\ of\ goods\ sold}{Revenues} \times 100$)

By doing this we eliminate the size effect and standardize the statement to facilitate comparison in terms of its past performance and also in comparison of other companies in the industry.
By combining common size analysis with profitability ratios, we can come up with some very quick insights into the performance of the company.

Two major components of that analysis are the gross profit margin ($= \frac{Gross\ profit}{Revenues} \times 100$), and net profit margin Net profit margin= $\frac{Net\ profit}{Revenues} \times 100$.

Gross profit margin is generally an indicator of a company strategy. Now higher GP margin indicates lower costs which is desirable but an analyst must analyze why a company is different from its peer group.
Are they using a new technology so their production procedure becomes more efficient from others?

Net profit margin tells us how much money we are earning for every dollar of revenue. There are several components that can be manipulated to get higher NP. Analyst must consider them. Still lower NP is not desirable.

Let's convert income statement of ABC corporation ltd into common size

Sales	100 m
CGS	-20m
GP	80 m
Admin expenses	-1m
Selling expenses	-1m
Net profit	78 m

Common size income statement

Sales	(100/100) x100 =100%
CGS	(20/100) x100 =20%
GP	80%
Admin expenses	1%
Selling expenses	1%
Net profit	78%

LOS 23l: Describe, calculate and interpret comprehensive income.

LOS 23m: Describe other comprehensive income and identify major types of items included in it.

Under IFRS total comprehensive income is defined as the change in equity during the period resulting from transactions and other events than those resulting from transactions with owners in their capacity as owners.

Under US GAAP total comprehensive income is defined as the change in equity, net assets on the business enterprise during the period from transactions and other events and circumstances from non-owner sources.

We know that, Net income= revenues – expenses incurred in generation of those revenues.

But total comprehensive income is bigger than net income. It includes all changes in equity during a period except contributions by owners and distributions to owners. So

Total comprehensive = net income + other comprehensive income (non-reported items).

Other comprehensive income:

There are four major transactions that are included in other comprehensive income and not in net income.

- Gains and losses from foreign currency exchange.
- Adjustments to the minimum pension liability.
- Any unrealized gains or losses from cash flow hedging derivatives.
- Unrealized gains and losses from available for sale securities.

If reporting under IFRS the company may choose to hold an asset in their books at fair value rather depreciating it from a historical cost.

Re valuations in this regard would also be included in other comprehensive income.

Understanding Balance Sheets Study
Session 7

LOS 24a: Describe the elements of the balance sheet: Assets, liabilities and equity.

A balance sheet is also known as statement of financial position or the statement of financial condition.

It shows financial situation of a company at a single point in time. It shows what do a company own, owe and what are the owners claims on that company.

There are three basic elements of a balance sheet
Assets, liabilities and equity.

Assets: Resources owned by the company for future economic benefits. These resources are result of past transaction or events. These resources are expected to make inflows for company.

Liabilities: Obligations on a company resulted from past transactions or events. These are expected to make an outflow from company.

Equity: This is residual claims of owners in a company. Equity = Assets – liabilities. Equity is also called owner`s equity or shareholder`s equity. Sometimes it is also called net assets.

To make a balance sheet we need to follow basic balance sheet equation

Assets = Liabilities + Equity.

It means assets, which are resources owned by company are either financed by creating liabilities or by owner`s equity.

LOS 24 b: Describe uses and limitations of the balance sheet in financial analysis.

Balance sheet shows financial position of a company at a single point in time in terms of what a company own, owe and what claim the owners have. It shows the financial health of the company.

With the help of balance sheet, we can determine company`s liquidity position, solvency position and its ability to distribute cash to the owners. Liquidity means firm`s ability to meet short term obligations. Solvency means firm`s ability to meet long term obligations.

Limitations of balance sheet: A company`s balance sheet does not necessarily reflect its intrinsic market value because of the three major reasons.

1. <u>Mixed valuation methods</u>. Assets and liabilities are measured using different methods of valuation. Some reported on historical cost, some fair value and the overall picture shows the judgment of the management which is not necessarily a reflection of how the market values them.

2. <u>Single point in time:</u> The balance sheet is reported at a single point in time. It means even the stated value of assets will only be accurate if the report is released when those valuations apply. After some time, they may be out of dated.

3. <u>Other factors:</u> There are significant numbers of factors that affect the company's value and not all of them are considered and shown on the balance sheet. For example, customer and employee`s loyalty good relations with suppliers etc.

LOS24c: Describe alternative formats of balance sheet presentation.

There are two styles for balance sheet presentation,
1. Classified style
2. Liquidity based style
   IFRS and US GAAP allows classified style but Liquidity base style is only permitted under IFRS.

Classified style: In this style, a company's accounts are separated into current and non-current assets and current and non-current liabilities.

Liquidity based style: In this method, we present the accounts in order of liquidity. We still have the distinction between assets, liabilities and equity but (rather than classifying items in terms of their current or non-current nature) we order all accounts under their broader categories in terms of liquidity. This style is more often used in banking.

LOS 24d: Distinguish between current and non-current assets and current and non-current liabilities.

Current assets: An item is current asset if it fulfills any of following conditions
- An instrument held for trading.
- An item that is expected to be sold in either a year or one operating cycle whichever is longer.
- An item that is expected to be used in either a year or one operating cycle whichever is longer. Or
- An item that somehow is expected to be converted into cash in either a year or one operating cycle whichever is longer.
   Current assets are usually orders in balance sheet according to their liquidity. More liquids are at first position like cash. Current assets reveled operating activities of a firm.

Operating cycle: It is the time period from the purchase of goods or materials through the sale of the product and the collection of cash.

None-current assets: These are assets that are not quickly convert into cash or used within one operating cycle (do not fulfill the conditions of current assets). These assets provide information about the company's investing activities.

Current liabilities: If any one of the following definitions for a liability is fulfilled we call it current liability.

- Liabilities held for trading,
- A liability expected to settle within a year or a single operating cycle is current
- For a liability to be current, the company must not have the unconditional right to push it into next period.

Non-current liabilities:

For a liability If any of the above-mentioned characteristics are not fulfilled, then we have a non-current liability. These are longer term obligations and reveals about firm`s investing activities.

LOS 24e: Describe different types of assets and liabilities and the measurement bases of each.

Part 1: Assets.

Current assets: These are the assets which will be used in one operating cycle or within one year, whichever is longer. Some common current assets are

Cash and cash equivalents: These are the most liquid current assets. It is places at top in current assets. Under cash and cash equivalents we have cash balance held at banks and short-term instruments like a U. S. treasury bill which can be easily and quickly converted into cash and have minimal interest rate risk. These are held at fair value or at amortized cost. These are considered financial assets.

Marketable securities. It means Investments with a little more risk than cash equivalents. Normally in this section we have publicly traded debt and equity securities like government securities, notes, bonds etc.

Trade receivables: These are the sum of amount due on accounts from customers that arise from sale of goods and or services rendered.

Receivables provide us useful information about company's relationship with their customers. Does company have a diversified group of buyers or are they concentrated and dependent on a small group. Trade receivables (also called account receivables) are held at net realizable value. Net realizable value= gross receivables – provision for bad debts. The amount of bad debts provision must be closer to industry norms. Because the management can under value this provision to overstate the earnings.

Inventory: Raw material, work in process and finished products come in this category. It is important to note that not every company have things like this in inventory because not every firm manufacture and sell. With inventory analysis we must understand the business of that company.

Certain costs can also be included in the value of inventory like, purchase price, cost involved in bringing the inventory to usable location in a useable condition. Some costs cannot be included in inventory value like, abnormal waste of material or labor etc., storage costs (if storage is crucial i.e. for perishable goods, it is included), the administrative overheads, selling costs.

Under IFRS inventory must be held in the balance sheet at the lower of cost or net realizable value. <u>Net realizable value</u> = estimated selling price - costs of completion - any costs incurred in making a sale.

Under U. S. GAAP valuation is based on the lower of cost or market. Market is normally equal to replacement cost. It cannot be greater than net realizable value and also
Market < net realizable value - normal profit margin.
Important: Under IFRS if the value of inventory is written down and then afterwards value rises we can adjust the value of the account upwards.
U. S. GAAP does not allow award reversal of inventory.

<u>Two methods to value inventory:</u> **Standard costing method:** It takes into account materials and labor. This method is used by manufacturing firm and they assign predetermined cost of raw material, labor and overhead. **Retail method** means using gross margin and sales value to estimate cost.

Continuing with current assets we have;
Prepayments: Operating expenses that a company has paid in advance. It means we pay an expense in a different period to the period when the expense is actually incurred. We have cash outflow in one year but the corresponding expense will show up in the next year. In this case we create a current asset and write it down as it is used. For example prepaid insurance etc.

Deferred tax assets: Two ways to present deferred tax asset.
First, we can bring forward tax assets from periods where we made a net loss to offset the tax bills on periods where we have net profits.
Secondly, we may be required to report a certain amount of income for tax purposes.
Guiding the figure for taxes payable.
The same time we might have a figure for tax expense which is driven by the amount of income we have chosen to recognize in that period. The actual amount of tax paid is higher than the reported tax expense that we will be able to carry a deferred tax asset forward into the next period.

Non-current assets

Property plant and equipment: Any property intended to use for administrative purposes or the production of goods or services would be included in plant property and equipment (PP&E). PP&E are tangible assets that are expected to provide economic benefits over multiple periods.

Under IFRS PP&E is reported using cost or revaluation model.

U. S. GAAP only allows the cost model.

1. Cost model: This is the carrying value of asset on the balance sheet which is amortized cost of the asset. Amortized cost = historical cost of the asset - accumulated depreciation -impairment loss- depletion - amortization. **Historical cost** =all costs from purchasing plus the cost involved by getting the asset into working.

Depreciation is the distribution of asset`s cost over multiple periods. If there is a sudden and unexpected change in value it might not accurately reflect the value of an asset

To deal with sudden changes in value there is another concept called **impairment loss.** This account is created to reflect the sudden drop in value when carrying value of an asset > asset`s recoverable value.

Recoverable value: An asset`s recoverable amount is the higher of its fair value less cost to sell or its value in use.

It is the amount of cash we can get by selling the asset in arm's length transaction.

Value in use = present value of expected future cash flows of asset.

If after impairment loss, there is recovery it can be recorded under IFRS but US GAAP does not allow recovery.

After cost model we have revaluation model.

2. Revaluation model: Property plant and equipment is recorded at fair value minus accumulated depreciation. Any change in fair value must affect shareholder`s equity. Some times change in fair value also recorded in income statement.

Next in non-current assets we have

Investment property:

Any property in a company`s possession for investment purpose to gain financial benefits from rental income or capital appreciation is investment property.

IFRS allows us to use either the cost model or the fair value model to report investment property. When using fair value model any change in fair value will be reported in income statement.

U. S. GAAP does not offer specific guidance here.

Intangible assets: Intangible assets are defined as non-monetary assets having no physical existence.

For example, good will and trademarks.

IFRS allows us to use either the cost model or the revaluation model where US GAAP only permits the cost model.

There are two types of intangible assets.

Intangible assets with finite life: we amortize these as normal. It means we systematically allocate value of the asset to the available years of useful life and also account for unexpected changes in value. (as we did for property plant and equipment using impairment)

Intangible assets with indefinite lives: We do not amortize these assets but we test the value annually and write down in case of impairment. For example, Good will.

Part two, Liabilities:

Current liabilities:

These are the liabilities which will be satisfied (paid) in one operating cycle or in one year, whichever is longer. Following are most common current liabilities.

Trade payables: These are the payables of firm for goods and or services, the company has purchased on credit. There are various ways in which this figure can be interpreted. Increasing tendency in payables might tell us that firm is taking advantage of the available credit opportunities and reducing the short-term borrowings.

On the other hand, it may reflect that relationships between supplier and the company are getting worse. An analyst must look for sudden changes and if that happens he should investigate further.

Notes payable: It means financial borrowings payable within a year or in an operating cycle. Notes payables may include short term borrowing from, banker trade creditors. It also includes current portion of long term debt (interest payable).

Accrued liabilities: These are expenses that have been recognized but have not yet paid. This can include accrued expenses, income tax payable, interest payable, wages payable and other non-financial liabilities.

Unearned revenue: Revenues the company has taken in but not earned yet. It means the service has not yet been provided or the goods not yet delivered but inflow of cash has occurred. For example advance receipts from customer.

Non-current liabilities:

These are obligation not be satisfied in one operating cycle or one year. Following are some common non-current liabilities.

Long term financial liabilities: it means financial obligations that a company owes, are not expected to settle in one operating cycle or one year. For example, loan obtained for 5 years or a long-term bond. These must be held in balance sheet on amortized cost.

Deferred tax liabilities: It is the income tax payable in future as result of taxable temporary differences.

Deferred tax liability is created when tax expense recognized is greater than tax payable. A very good example for this is when a company chose to use accelerated depreciation for tax purpose but uses straight line method for financial reporting.

Using accelerated depreciation method, the depreciation expense will be higher in first periods and the tax payable would be less. Off course the tax payable would be higher in later periods. For this company choose to recognize higher tax payable in first periods so the affect will be offset in coming years.

LOS 24f: Describe the components of shareholder`s equity.

There are six components of owner's equity.
1. Contributed capital
2. Preferred stock
3. Treasury stock
4. Cumulated other comprehensive income
5. Non-controlling interests
6. Retained earnings.

1. Contributed capital: Also known as issued capital. The capital contributed by the owners. The company issue common stock in return for the contributed capital. Number of authorized, issued and outstanding shares must be disclosed on the company's balance sheet under equity. **Authorized shares** are the number of shares which can be issued under company`s article of incorporation. **Issued shares** are the number of shares issued to public. **Outstanding shares** are the issued shares minus number of shares company has purchased back (if any).

2. Preferred stock: Preferred stock holders have higher seniority than common shares. When a company is liquidated or issues dividend, preferred stock holders are paid first. Preferred stock holders get dividends at specific rate usually as a percentage of par value. But they do not have any voting right.

Preferred stocks can be classified as equity or a financial liability depending on the circumstances. If preferred stock are perpetual and non-redeemable shares (cannot be bought back by company), then they are classified as equity. If they are redeemable on a fixed date at a certain price, they would be classed as a financial liability. When a company repurchases their own shares, they can hold or cancel them. When they hold shares those are called **treasury stock**. Company can resell them in future if they hold them.

There are following reasons why a company buy its own stock
1. Management thinks shares are undervalued.
2. Shares are needed to meet employee stock option obligations.
3. Company wants to reduce or offset the dilution effect.

3. Treasury stock is not considered for votes or dividend.

4. Accumulated other comprehensive income: The accumulated value of Income Company has earned but not recognized as part of net income on their income statement because these revenues are not from ordinary business activities. These are changes in stockholder`s equity other than net income and owner`s contribution like dividends payments, issuing stock).

5. Retained earnings: Company`s incomes that have not been paid out in dividends.

LOS24g: Convert balance sheets to common size balance sheets and interpret common size balance sheets.

Divide the amount of each item on balance sheet by the amount of total assets and multiply result by 100. For example, if cash account is $10,000, divide $10,000 by total assets and then multiply by 100. [$(1000/total\ assets)\, x100$].
Do the same with other items like inventory, notes payable PP&E and bank loan etc.

Interpreting common size balance sheet:
First of all, we should look at the firm`s liquidity position. It means how their current assets are, compared to the current liabilities as a percentage of total assets. More percentage of current asset is, the better.
Secondly, we need to analyze the firm's **cash position** compared to current liabilities. Do we have enough cash to meet near term obligations if not then the company will have to pull in some cash from the sale of inventory (which is a bad sign).

Inventory: High levels of inventory percentage shows the company is potentially risking obsolescence and low level indicate the potential risk of stock shortage. Ideally these percentages must be close to industry norms or peer groups.

Now let's talk about the company's ability to meet long term obligations [long term liabilities/total assets] ? What portion of total assets are financed or represented by long term debt. Higher level of long term debt as a proportion of total assets indicates that the company is not going to meet long term obligations and have risk of insolvency.

LOS24h: Calculate and interpret liquidity and solvency ratios.

Liquidity based ratios: Measures firm's ability to meet short term obligations. But these ratios must not be considered in isolation. They must be considered collectively.

Current ratio: = current assets / current Liabilities. It measures how many times a firm has current assets to meet current liabilities. A ratio of 1 or higher is desirable. One drawback of current ratio is that the makeup of current assets could be very different from company to company. So, the current ratio could be very misleading. For example, if firm has more inventory and less cash the current ratio might be greater than one but this situation is not ideal (as inventory is not considered a great source of finance in short term).

To cover this flaw, we have **quick ratio** which consider more liquid assets. Quick ratio = {Cash + marketable securities + receivables} / Current liabilities.

Cash ratio= {cash + marketable securities} / current liabilities.

Solvency ratios:

Long term debt to equity ratio = the total amount of long term debt / total equity.

Total debt to total equity ratio = total debt / total equity

Debt ratio = total debt / total assets.

Financial leverage = total assets / total equity.

These ratios show company's ability to meet long term obligations. We need to look at trends in these ratios from a company's historical figures to assess company's performing over time. We can use these ratios to compare with peer group. But these ratios must also be considered collectively.

Understanding Cash flow Statements
Study session 7

LOS 25a: Compare cash flows from operating, investing and financing activities and classify cash flow items as relating to one of those three categories given a description of the items.

In this LOS, we need to understand the difference among three parts of Cash flow. These three parts are
1. **CFO** cash flow from operations.
2. **CFI** cash flow from investing activities.
3. **CFF** cash flow from financing activities.

CFO cash flow from operations: In this heading, we have all cash-based transactions that affect the company's net income. It means day to day inflows and outflows, related to the company`s ordinary business activities.
An example of inflows: Incoming cash received from customers. Proceeds of selling securities held for trading.
Outflows: Cash paid to employees or vendors. Acquisition of the securities etc.
Under IFRS
Interest received and interest paid can be classified as either operating or financing activity.
With dividends, IFRS offers us the choice between CFO and CFI.
Under US GAAP Interest and dividends received and interest paid are also classified as operating but dividends paid is not a component of CFO under U. S. GAAP. U. S. GAAP classifies dividends paid as a financing activity.

CFI cash flow from investing activity: In terms of inflows, Proceeds from the sale of non-trading securities or assets like plant property and equipment or intangible assets.
Out flows: Cash payments to bring these kinds of assets into the firm.

CFF Cash flow from financing: These are Cash flows related to the firm's capital structure.
 Inflows may include money received from the issuance of equity our bonds or cash borrowed.

Outflows: Money used to re purchase common stock. Paying a bond or paying other borrowings.

LOS 25b: Describe how non-cash investing and financing activities are reported.

Since there is no cash changing hands in this kind of transaction, it's not going to be recorded in cash flow statement but need to be disclosed either in footnotes to the financials are in a supplementary disclosure.

LOS 25.c: Contrast cash flow statements prepared under International Financial Reporting Standards (IFRS) and US generally accepted accounting principles (US GAAP).

Under IFRS
Interest received and interest paid can be classified as either operating or financing activity. In terms of dividends IFRS offers us the choice between CFO and CFI.

Under US GAAP Interest and dividends received and interest paid are also classified as operating but dividends paid is not a component of CFO under U. S. GAAP.U. S. GAAP classifies dividends paid as a financing activity.

Another difference between these two is in form of income tax paid. Under US GAAP all taxes paid are reported as operating activities, even the tax is related to financing or investing activities. Under IFRS income tax is operating activity but if the tax is related to financing or investing activities, it is reported there (not in operating activities).

LOS25d: Distinguish between the direct and indirect methods of presenting cash from operating activities and describe arguments in favor of each method.

We have two methods to present cash flow statement, the direct method and the indirect method.
CFI is same in these two methods. Choice of method only affects CFO and CFF.

Direct method: In this method, we take the accrual-based income statement line by line and convert it into a cash-based report. We start from the top of the income statement and go down through line by line.

Example of direct method

XYX corporation
Operating cash flow statement – Direct method
For the year ended 31 Dec. 2x18

Cash received from customers*	10000
(less) Cash paid to suppliers	2000
(less) Cash paid for Operating expenses	1000
(less) Cash paid for interest	100
(less) Cash paid for taxes	150
Operating cash flow	6750

*Cash received from customers= sales + Decrease in account receivables - Increase in account receivables

Indirect method: In this method we start with net income and make adjustments to eliminate non-cash elements of the income statement like depreciation and amortization to get operating cash flow.

Let's discuss how do changes in the balance sheet affect cash flow from operations.

There's a direct relationship between how assets/ liabilities change and cash changes.

When an asset`s account increases or a liability account decreases that indicates that the company is using cash.

On the other hand, when an asset account decreases or a liability account increases that's cash is coming into company (source of cash).

Example of indirect method of cash flow statement
XYX Corporation
Operating cash flow statement-Indirect method
For the year ended 31 Dec. 2x19

Net Income	500 0
Add Depreciation expense	100
Add Amortization	100
Less Increase in Account receivables	50
Less increase in inventory	100
Add Decrease in prepaid expenses	200 0
Less decrease in account payables	250

Less decrease in accrued liabilities	50
Operation cash flow	675
	0

Notice the operating Cash flow will remain same in any method.

Reasons for using direct method or indirect

The direct method shows us cash receipts and cash payment separately where the indirect method only shows us the net cash flow so direct method provides us more information.

On the other hand, indirect method gives us a valuable insight into the relationship between a company's income and their operating cash flow when building cash flow forecasts. So, the indirect method is more helpful to an analyst in terms of forecasting but direct method is more informative.

LOS25e: Describe how the cash flow statement is linked to the income statement and the balance sheet.

Link between cash flow statement and the balance sheet. Cash is an asset on the balance sheet reported at a specific date. Consecutive balance sheets tell us the cash balances at the beginning and the end of a period. Cash flow statement explains how the change occurred in between.

Relationship between cash flow, the balance sheet and the income statement: We need to look at individual asset or liability account separately. For example, if a company is selling goods we need to look how much of the cash is received and how much goes into receivables. By selling we get revenues which come into income statement. Receivables go into balance sheet while cash in the cash flow statement along with balance sheet.

Another relationship could be established between changing payables and cash flow statement, income statement and balance sheet. If the purchases are greater than the cash paid, we know that the payables will increase.

LOS25f: Describe the steps in the preparation of direct and indirect cash flow statements, including how cash flows can be computed using income statement and balance sheet data.

Remember that regardless of the choice of direct or indirect CFI and CFF will be the same. Only CFO is affected by direct or indirect method.

Direct method: Under this method, net cash flows from operating activities are calculated by taking cash receipts from sales, adding interest and dividends received, and deducting cash payments for purchases, operating expenses, interest and income taxes.

Cash collections: From Account receivables, we take the opening receivables plus sale revenues minus closing balance of receivables and the resulting amount would be cash collected. In case of unearned revenues, add the opening balances of receivables and unearned revenue and add the closing balances of receivables and unearned revenue and proceed as normal.

Cash payments: We need to look at 1. Cash paid to suppliers and 2. cash paid to employees.
Cash paid to suppliers is just like cash collections. Just look at how the payables accounts changes over the period and how much of that change is because of the purchase is bigger from the income statement.
opening payables + purchases - ending balance of payables = cash paid out to suppliers.

If we are not given purchase figure but given inventory and cost of goods sold. In this case we need to calculate purchases by following formula
(Ending inventory - Beginning inventory) + Cost of goods sold = Inventory purchases

Cash paid to employees: Look for wages payable changes (balance sheet figure) and wages expense (in the income statement).
opening balance of wages payable + wages expense (current) - ending balance = cash paid to employees.

Operating expenses: Start with the operating expenses from the income statement. We need to adjust from accrual base to cash base. Increase in prepayments shows use of cash. Increase in accrued liabilities indicates a source of cash. It means we have not paid so we have delayed the outflow.
Cash paid for interest.
Cash paid for tax.
Remember depreciation is non-cash expense so we ignore it in direct method.

CFO by the indirect method:
1. Take the company's net income.
2. Remove any cash flow related to financing or investing activity because they are non operating expenses. They will come under CFI and CFF.
3. Add any non-cash expense and minus any non-cash revenue.
4. Account for the sources and uses of cash as reflected in the changes to balance the accounts. When an asset increases it means we used cash so subtract the

change. When an asset decreases the change is added. When a liability increases we delayed cash so add the change while a decrease in liability, means we used cash so subtract the change.
5. Any losses incurred in the sale of assets, any losses experienced in the sale of investments are added back because they are from investing activities. All the gains from these items must be subtracted.

6. Add all non-cash items like depreciation or amortization (of intangibles and bond discount).

Changes in the balance sheet

In this section we will see how operating assets and liabilities change from period to period.

Operating assets are receivables, inventory prepayments, deferred tax assets etc. Operating liabilities are payables, both trade payables and internal payables, accrued expenses and deferred tax liabilities.

Add back any decreases in operating assets or increases in operating liabilities because they are sources of cash. And subtract any increase in operating asset or decrease in operating liabilities because these are uses of cash.

Now have a look at CFI and CFF

Investing activities:
We need to figure out how much money was spent during the period on new asset. For that we need to look at the change in the asset account.

How much was the balance of the asset at the beginning of the period and how much was there at the end.

Ending balance of asset can be calculated as,
Beginning value of asset + money paid out for assets - money received in for assets sold = ending balance.

For each asset sold we need to consider both the book value of the asset and the gain or loss on the sale. If the sale gave us gain, we need to add that amount to the book value. A loss would have to be removed from the book value to get to the cash proceeds on the sale.

CFF financing activities: This includes transactions related to the company's capital structure. we need to look at the company's interactions with their creditors and their shareholders. With the creditors we may have inflows like the issuance of new debt. And outflows like repayment of existing debt. For the shareholders we have inflows from equity issuance and we have outflows for dividends and stock repurchase.

So, for creditors the net effect on cash flow could be represented like this.
New borrowings - any principal repaid. We are only looking at principal repaid because we are assuming that we have covered interest payments as part of CFO under IFRS.
For the shareholders we have equity issued inflows minus outflows for share repurchase and dividends paid.

LOS25g: Convert cash flows from the indirect to direct method.

CFI and CFF would be identical regardless of which method is chosen so we focus only on CFO.
Reason to convert from the indirect method to the direct method: CFO constructed by the direct method is a more valuable resource for an analyst than constructed by indirect method.

There are three steps of this conversion.
1. Disaggregate net income into total revenues and total expenses. And take totals of net revenues and total expenses separately (the income statement and balance sheet will be given).

We simply take the income statement for incomes and take a total and then separate out the expenses and take a total the net between those two figures should equal net income.
2. Disaggregated these two figures into their cash and non-cash components. Separate none cash revenues from revenues and separate none cash expenses from expenses.
3. Take the two cash components and built CFO using direct method from scratch. That means we're talking about cash collected from customers, cash paid to suppliers and employees operating expenses interest and tax.

LOS 25h: Analyze and interpret both reported and common size cash flow statements.

In this section we are going to understand company's cash flow situation.

Major sources and uses of cash: The uses and sources of cash of a firm is important part of cash flow analysis. When a firm is at start it most probably be generating negative cash flow from operations and this might be financed by external sources of cash like investing and or financing activities. After sometimes when the company is establishing itself it must generate positive cash flows from operating activities so it can return the external financing.

Operating cash flow:
First of all, we look at the trends in working capital. Cash flow statements constructed by indirect method show us how current assets (like inventory, receivables, payables, etc.) are changing over time and this will give us a great idea of how operating cash flows changing and why.

Interpretation: A positive operating cash flow is good if it is generated from operating activities. But positive cash flow is not good if it is being generated by selling current assets like inventory.

One important thing to note is that a cash flow figure higher (lower) than the net income indicates good (bad/ aggressive/ improper accounting) reporting quality.

Cash flow from Investing activities: We need to consider each line item individually and find out what we have in uses of cash and sources of cash.

Uses of cash: Spending money on property plant and equipment or maybe we are acquiring companies for cash or investing in securities of other companies.

Sources of cash: Sources of cash in investing activities may be sale of property plant and equipment, selling of a business unit etc.

Interpretation: The important thing to note with sales is, why is the company selling assets. Are they selling to invest in a better opportunity or they are generating cash to meet obligations?

Cash flow from financing activity:
This is also study of the uses and sources of cash.

Uses of cash: The Company may be repurchasing their own stock or paying dividends to equity shareholders.

Sources of cash: Sources of cash in CFI might be issuance of debt or equity issuance. An analyst must examine why the company has a positive or negative cash flow here.

Interpretation: An outflow means negative balance which might be a good thing if company is paying off debts but an inflow (positive balance) might be a bad thing if the company needs to generate cash from financing activities to pay dividends. If this is the case it means company`s CFO are not sufficient.

Common size analysis of the cash flow statement:

Just like the income statement and balance sheet, common size analysis of cash flow statement can also be useful in understanding the company's cash flow. We have 2 methods for developing the common size cash flow statement.

1. The inflow/outflow method (revenue-based method). 2. The percentage sales method (as we did with income statement)

1. The inflow/outflow method (revenue-based method): we take each inflow as a percentage of the total inflow and each out flow as a percentage of the total outflow.
   This method shows where the concentration of cash inflow/outflow is. It is helpful to identify trends and future forecasting.

2. The percentage sales method: We simply take each line item as a percentage of sales revenue from the income statement. It is helpful to identify trends and future forecasting.

LOS25i: Calculate and interpret free cash flow to the firm, free cash flow to equity, and performance and coverage cash flow ratios.

Free cash flow (FCF): Free cash flow is the cash left after making capital expenditure (including growth). FCF is a measure of a company's financial performance, calculated as operating cash flow minus capital expenditures.
Two types of free cash flow. 1. Free cash flow to the firm and 2. free cash flow to equity.

1.Free cash flow to the firm: It is the cash available for both equity and debt holders. It means the cash available for dividends and interest payments after deduction of operating expenses and capital investment.
We calculate FCFC from operating cash flow as follow

FCFF = Cash Flow from Operations + Interest Expense x (1 - Tax Rate) – Capital expenditures. Remember that we need to add back in the interest expense (and eliminate the tax rate effect).

From net income we can calculate free cash by using following formula.

FCFF = net income + non-cash charges + interest x (1 - tax rate) - long-term investments - investments in working capital

We take net income add back non-cash charges like depreciation and amortization again add back the after-tax interest expense and then we remove capital expenditure and working capital investment. The result would be same from both formulae.

Free cash flow to equity: The cash available just to the equity holders. It is the cash left after operating expenses fixed capital investment and borrowing costs. It shows how much cash is available to the equity shareholders of the company as dividends or stock buybacks, after all expenses, reinvestments, and debt repayments.

Calculation of FCFE: **FCFE= CFO -net capital expenditure + net borrowings**
Where Net borrowing = Debt issued – debt paid.

Cash flow ratios:
We are to discuss performance and coverage ratios.

Performance ratios:

Cash flow to revenue ratio: **Formula;** Cash flow to revenue ratio = CFO/ net revenues.
It tells us how much cash is generated per dollar of revenue.

Cash return on assets: **Formula:** CFO/ Average total assets. It tells us how much cash is generated per dollar of assets.

Cash return on equity: **Formula:** CFO/ Average shareholder`s equity.It tells us how much cash is generated per dollar of shareholders investment.

Cash flow to income ratio: **Formula:** CFO/ Operating income. It tells us the cash generating ability from operations.

Cash flow per share: **Formula;** (CFO – preferred dividend)/Weighted average number of common shares.

Coverage ratios

Debt coverage ratio: **Formula;** CFO/ Total debt. It tells us about company's financial risk and leverage.

Interest coverage ratio: **Formula;** (CFO + tax paid + interest paid)/ interest paid. It measures the company's ability to pay interest. Sometimes under IFRS interest paid is given under financing activity. Just take that interest and nothing else need to do.

Long term Debt repayment ratio: **Formula;** CFO/ cash paid on long term debt. It measures the company's ability to pay down debt obligations with operating cash flow.

Dividend payment ratio = CFO /dividends paid. It measures the company's ability to pay dividends out of operating cash.

Reinvestment ratio: formula; CFO/ Long term assets. It measures firm`s ability to acquire long term assets by using CFO.

The investing and financing ratio: Formula; CFO/ Cash outflow for investing and financing activities. It tells us about the firm`s ability to satisfy debts, pay dividends and asset purchase.

Financial analysis techniques
Study session 7

LOS 26a: Describe tools and techniques used in financial analysis, including their uses and limitations.

There are several tools and techniques which are used to convert financial statements into those formats which can be easily analyzed. These are ratio analysis, common size analysis, graphical analysis, regression analysis etc.

These tools are very importance when companies are not compatible because of different locations or maybe they operate in different industries.

Ratio analysis benefits: Ratio analysis is used for
- Internal and external comparison.
- To project future earnings and cash flow.
- To evaluate a company's financial flexibility (ability to obtain cash) to meet its obligations and to grow even in case of difficult financial circumstance.
- To measure the performance of a company's management.
- To look at how the company or the industry is changing over time.
- To compare company with their peer companies or relevant industry benchmarks.

Limitation of ratios: 1. They are not useful in isolation. They are only useful when they are combined with an overall understanding of the company the company's industry and the macroeconomic environment.
3. Ratio analysis is also not useful for big companies that have multiple sources of income from entirely different industries. Because of the complexity of the big company, relevant benchmarks won't be available.

4. Analysis based on small subset of ratios might not be reliable because one set of financial ratios might indicate a certain level of performance but another set of ratios on the same company might indicate that that performance level is not sustainable.
5. Ratios calculated from financial reports build on differing accounting standards may not be immediately comparable. (Accounting treatments differs in inventory evaluation, appreciation and off-balance sheet items.)

Common size analysis: Common size is all about expressing financial data or entire financial statements relative to a single item.

Vertical common size balance sheets base everything relative to total assets. So total assets would be marked in the report as a hundred percent and everything else is expressed as a percentage of that total assets figure. For example,

percentage of cash = $\dfrac{cash}{total\ asset} x100$

The benefits:
We can determine
- The company's financing sources. and
- How does the company's balance sheet differ from the industry norm.

Vertical common size income statements are very similar to a vertical common size balance sheet. In vertical common size income statement everything is calculated as percentage of total revenues. For example, Gross profit percentage = $\dfrac{Gross\ profit}{sales} x100$.

Vertical common size reports both balance sheet and income statement are useful to an analyst performing a cross sectional analysis. With cross sectional analysis we're comparing some metric of one company to that same metric from another company or to an industry benchmark.

For example, if one company has shown receivables on their vertical common size balance sheet thirty two percent of total assets but another company or all of the companies in the industry are below ten percent.

We need to know what this company is doing differently. This requires more investigation.

Horizontal common size statements state everything relative to a base year.

For example, if the total assets in the first year is a hundred twenty million dollars and in the next year they have total assets on the hundred and thirty million dollars.

The first year will be shown as a hundred percent with the second-year show is a hundred eight-point three percent. This format is useful for answering questions like how the relative position of the company is changing and how was their management of receivables and payable changing over time.

Horizontal common size statements are useful for trend analysis.

XYZ corp. LTD
Income statement
For the year ended 31Dec.2xx9
income statement

Vertical common size

Sales	1000	(1000/1000)x10000	100%
COGS	600	600/1000)x100	60%
GP	400	(400/1000)x100(40	40%
Operating	40	(40/1000)x100=	4%
Admin exp	30	(30/1000)x100=	3%
Tax Expense	10	(10/1000)x100=	1%
Netprofit	320	(320/1000)x100=	32%

XYZ corp. LTD
Balance sheet
As on 31Dec.2xx9

Year	2x x6	2x x7	2x x8	Horizontal common size balance sheet taking 2xx6 as base year		
				2xx6 (in %)	2xx7 (in %)	2xx8 (in %)
Assets						
Cash and cash equivalents	100	120	140	(100/100)x100= 100	(120/100)x100 = 120%	140
Account receivables	80	90	100	(80/80) x100=100	(90/80)x100=1 12.5	125
Inventory	200	210	220	100	105	110
PP&E	1000	1000	1000	100	100	100
Total assets	**1380**	**1420**	**1460**	**100**	102.89	105.79
Liabilities						
Account	10	10	11	100	105	110

payables	0	5	0			
Interest payable	50	55	60	100	110	120
long term debt	70 0	73 0	76 0	100	104.2857143	108.57 14
total liabilities	**85 0**	**89 0**	**93 0**	**100**	**104.71**	**109.41**
common equity	53 0	53 0	53 0	100	100	100
total liabilities & Equity	**13 80**	**14 20**	**14 60**	**100**	**102.89%**	**105.79**

Graphical analysis: Graphical analysis is building visual representations of financial information to aid in the understanding comparison or explanation of the company's financial performance. Some examples of graphical analysis tools are stocked bar graphs, pie charts and line graphs. Each useful in their own way for expressing information over different time periods and emphasizing different areas.

Regression analysis: Regression analysis is all about discovering a statistical relationship between two variables. (Details are not included in CFA curriculum)
Common example is sales to GDP. Can we draw a significantly consistent relationship between how company sales changes in relation to real GDP.

LOS 26b: Classify, calculate and interpret activity, liquidity, solvency, profitability and valuation ratios.

In this LOS we have to classify these ratios, calculate them and also interpret them.
We have five classifications of ratios.
1. Activity ratios: 2. Liquidity ratios   3. Solvency ratios   4. Profitability ratios 5. Valuation ratios.
Note: These classifications are not mutually exclusive.

Activity ratios

Activity ratios are also called asset utilization ratios or operating efficiency ratios. These ratios measure firm's ability to manage their assets. We have following ratios in this category.

Receivable turnover ratio: How efficiently a firm control receivable is measured by **receivable turnover ratio**.
Receivable turnover ratio = Annual sales/ average receivables.
This ratio should be closer to industry norms.

> One thing must be remembered here is that whenever we use balance sheet data with income statement or cash flow data in a ratio, the balance sheet figure must be taken as average by adding opening and ending balances and divided by 2.

Number of days sales are outstanding or average collection period: It is the average number of days taken by the customers to pay to the firm.
No. of days sales outstanding = 365/ receivable turnover
This ratio should be close to industry norms. If it is too high it means the firm is not collecting cash easily (inefficiency). A too low this ratio shows a very strict credit policy which might be affecting sales or the firm is collecting cash very efficiently.

Inventory turnover ratio= Cost of goods sold/ average inventory
It measures firm`s efficiency in inventory management and its processing. It tells how many times the firm has sold its inventory completely (theoretically).

Days inventory in hand = 365/ inventory turnover
It tells us how many days a firm takes to process its inventory. Again, these (Inventory turnover and Days inventory in hand) should be close to industry norms. A higher inventory turnover ratio means lesser days inventory in hand. It might indicate a highly effective inventory management or the company is not holding enough stock and is potentially on the verge of shortages and falling sales revenue. Analyst must see revenues growth to assess the explanation. A higher (or same as industry) growth with high turnover means effective inventory management and vice versa. A lower inventory turnover means higher number of days inventory in hand may indicate that there is too much capital is tied up and high processing time. It means inventory could be getting obsolete. The cost of goods sold may not be according to current circumstances.

Payable turnover ratio = purchases/ average payables: It means how many times company pays its payables completely (theoretically).
Number of days of payables= 365/ payable turnover ratio
These two should be close to industry norms. A relatively higher payables turnover (which would mean a relatively lower number of days payables are outstanding) the company might not be effectively taking advantage of credit facilities made available to them or they might be taking advantage of early payment discounts. We must look at the liquidity ratios to get proper understanding. If company has better liquidity ratios but higher days payable (lower payable turnover) it means they are taking advantage of available credit

facilities. If liquidity position is bad with lower payable turnover they might be having trouble with cash generation.

Working capital turn over = Total sales/ average working capital. Working capital is the difference between current assets and current liabilities.

It tells us how efficiently the company is turning their working capital investment into sales revenue. It indicates how much revenue the company is generating per dollar of working capital investment. For example, if working capital turnover is 5, it means for every dollar of working capital we generate five dollars of sales revenue. A zero or negative of this ratio is not useable.

The fixed asset turnover = Sales revenue by/ Average net fixed assets

It tells us how efficiently investment in fixed assets is being turned into sales revenue.

Interpretation: Higher figure would indicate efficient use of fixed assets. A lower number may indicate inefficiency in business because it requires a large capital investment. Or it is a newborn company that has not yet reached at its full capacity.

Total asset turnover = Sales revenue / average total assets

It tells us how efficiently the company is generating revenue from their assets.

Interpretation: A higher figure indicates that the company is effectively or efficiently utilizing their assets to generate revenue. Lower figure would indicate inefficiencies or the firm is in very capital-intensive business.

Liquidity ratios

Liquidity ratios measure a company's ability to meet its short-term obligations.

We have 3 major liquidity ratios, the current ratio, the quick ratio and the cash ratio.

Current ratio= Current assets /current liabilities.

Quick ratio= Liquid assets / current liabilities. Where, Liquid assets = cash+ marketable sec. + receivables

Cash ratio = (cash + marketable securities) / current liabilities.

Interpretations

A current ratio of one indicates that the company's current assets are equals the dollar value of their current liabilities. So, the short-term obligations are just covered. A ratio less than one means that the company is relying on operating profit to meet short term obligations because current assets are not enough.

Same interpretation is for following ratios too.

Quick ratio is more realistic approach about our ability to convert certain current assets into cash. Pre-payments for example might be included in the current assets of a company but would be are very difficult to turn into cash. Same is the case with inventory. So, we exclude these two in quick ratio to have more meaningful results.

With cash ratio we are more conservative about the asset`s ability to meet short-term obligations. We only include most liquid assets. We only include cash and marketable securities the company has right now to pay their short term obligations.

Other liquidity ratios the defensive interval and the cash conversion cycle.

Defensive interval = (cash + marketable securities + receivables)/ average daily expenditures

It is a measure of how long the company can continue paying its liabilities with current assets assuming no new inflows.

For example, a defensive interval of 40 means the company can survive the current pace for 40 days without getting any cash inflow. Higher number indicates greater liquidity.

Cash conversion cycle = {(days sales outstanding) +days inventory in hand) – (Number of days of payables)}

It is the time company takes to turn a product into cash (from inventory to receivable to cash collection).

A shorter time means greater liquidity. It should be compared with industry norms.

Solvency ratios:

Solvency ratios measure a company's ability to meet longer term obligations. This category is most relevant to analysts interested in a company's financial leverage and their ability to service long term debt.

Solvency ratios typically have two categories.

1. Debt ratios   2. Coverage ratios.

Debt ratios

Debt to equity =Total debt / total equity.

This ratio compares the debt side of the capital structure to the equity side. It shows how much debt a company is using to finance its assets in comparison to equity. A higher figure would indicate a less solvent company.

Debt to assets ratio= total debt / total assets.

This ratio compares the company's debt position to the value of their total assets. It tells us the percentage of total assets financed by debt (all liabilities). A higher ratio indicates weak solvency.

Debt to capital ratio= Total debt / (total debt + shareholders equity).

Total debt means all interest bearing short and long-term debt. Equity includes common stock and preferred stock. It shows how much of capital is financed by debt. A higher ratio indicates weak solvency.

Financial leverage= Average total assets / average total equity.

A higher ratio here indicates the company is using a higher proportion of debt to finance their assets which indicates risk.

Coverage ratios

There are two major coverage ratios, interest coverage ratio and the fixed charge coverage ratio.

Interest coverage ratio= EBIT/interest payment

EBIT is earning before interest and taxes. It measures how many times a company's earnings before interest and tax covers their interest obligations.

A higher number is desirable here because it indicates that the earnings are quite bigger than interest payment. A lower of this ratio means they have difficulty in payment of interest.

Fixed charge coverage = (EBIT + lease payments) / (interest expense plus lease payments).

It tells us how well the company's fixed outflows are covered by their earning. A higher ratio indicates the company is in a better position and vice versa.

Profitability ratios

Profitability ratios measure the overall performance of the firm in terms of revenues, assets, capital and equity.

Before the profitability ratios we need a good understanding of the structure of the income statement.

Net sales revenue - cost of goods sold = gross profit.

gross profit -operating expenses = operating profit EBIT = earnings before interest and taxes

EBIT- interest = earnings before tax= EBT

EBT- taxes = earnings after tax.

Earning after tax – other items = net income before dividends.

Total capital = long term debt + short term debt + common equity + preferred equity.

Some analysts may use total assets for total capital if they want to include things like accounts payable.

No let's look at the profitability ratio.

We have two categories of profitability ratios

1. Ratios based on the company's sales revenue   2. Ratios based on capital invested.

Ratios based on the company's sales revenue

Gross profit margin = gross profit / revenues.

Gross profit margin indicates the number of sales left over after counting for the cost of goods sold. It is a comparison of Gross profit with sales. A higher gross profit margin indicates company's ability to charge a higher price for a product they can manufacture for a lower cost and vice versa. Gross profit margin also helps the management in cost control.

Operating profit margin = Operating profit / sales revenues.

We know that operating profit is gross profit minus operating costs. While analyzing operating profit margin it's a custom to compare the trend of operating Margin with gross margin.

If operating profit margin is improving faster than gross profit margin then the company may be getting more efficient to bring down the operating cost.

Pretax margin = earnings before tax / sales revenue.

This is another measure of profitability. An analyst should be careful to consider whether the item driving a change in pretax margin is likely to continue into the future or if it's a onetime event (due to non-recurring items).

Ratios based on capital invested
Return on assets =Net income / average total assets.

It tells us how much income the company has earned per dollar of assets. This is a better measure of how they performed by taking their size into consideration. The main problem with this ratio is that net income is a return for only equity holders (both common and preferred) but for most companies, assets are financed by both equity and debt.

To eliminate this drawback and account for debt holder`s profitability an analyst might use operating return on assets, calculated as

ROA= (Net income + interest expense (1-tax rate)} / average total assets.

Return on total capital= EBIT/Average total capital

Total capital is short and long-term debt and common and preferred equity. In this ratio we measure the return on per dollar of capital invested. A very low of this ratio from industry norms should alarm the analyst.

Return on equity (or return on total equity) = Net income / average total equity.

This ratio focuses on the equity holders including preferred equity. It should also be according to industry norms. A very low of this ratio must concern analyst.

Return on common equity = Net income – preferred dividends)/average common equity

While net income – preferred dividends is equal to income available to common stock holders.

This ratio measures the return just to the common shareholders and compares that figure to the capital invested by just the common shareholders.

Valuation ratios

Valuation ratios are all about ownership and the benefit of ownership. These ratios are ratios like price to earnings price to cash flow price to sales price to book value.

This stuff is all covered later on in the equity material and even some of it later on in this section.

LOS 26 c: Describe relationships among ratios and evaluate a company using ratio analysis.

Let's have an example to relate ratios and company evaluation.

Sample balance sheet

Year	Current	Previous
Assets	000$	000$
Cash and equivalent	50	40

Trade receivables	70	60
inventory	210	200
total current assets	**330**	**300**
property plant ad equipment	2000	2000
Accumulated depreciation	300	295
Net property plant and equipment	1700	1720
Total assets	**2030**	**2020**
Liabilities		
Trade payables	114	113
Current portion of long term debt	70	65
Short term debt	130	125
Total current liabilities	**314**	**295**
Long term debt	590	610
Deferred tax	116	110
Common stock at par	260	260
Additional paid up capital	500	500
Retained earnings	250	245
Total shareholders equity	1010	1005
Total liabilities and equity	**2030**	**2020**

Sample income statement

Year	Current	previous
Sales	10000	**9500**
Cost of goods sold	9000	8600
Gross profit	1000	900
Operating expenses	560	540
EBIT	440	360
Interest expense	40	35

EBT	400		325
Taxes	55		52
Net income	345		273
Common dividend	245		173

Ratios	Current	Previous	Industry benchmark
Current ratio	1.05	**1.016949153**	1.1
Quick ratio	0.38	0.338983051	1
cash ratio	0.1592357	0.169491525	0.7
inventory turnover	43.902439	41.95121951	42
days inventory in hand	8.3138889	8.700581395	8
receivable turnover	153.84615	146.1538462	150
days sales outstanding	2.3725	2.497368421	1.5

Now let's look at what these ratios are telling us about this company.

Firstly, in terms of the current ratio.

The current ratio is increasing which suggests that current assets are increasing relative to current liabilities. Meaning that the company is improving their liquidity position. Moreover, it is also close to industry benchmark.

But the quick ratio doesn't look so good. Although it has increased slightly but still very low from industry bench mark. It tells us that we do not have sufficient more liquid assets.

If we have only two ratios it is fair to comment that the company`s liquidity is not good and inventory is misleading its current ratio.

No if we bring in the days sales outstanding figures we just calculated we can see a decline from 2.4 days to 2.3 days. This is suggesting that the company is collecting cash on their receivables a bit quicker than they were before which is a positive sign but it is still greater than industry.

Days inventory in hand is also improving and is very close to industry norms.

Putting all of that together it looks like although this company's inventory and receivable ratios are good but their liquidity position is actually weakening.

LOS 26d: Demonstrate the application of DU Pont analysis of return on equity and calculate and interpret effects of changes in its components.

DuPont analysis: It is a method used to analyze a company's return on equity. In this we can use algebra to break the simple return on equity formula and find out what is driving return on equity.

The basic formula: *return on equity= Net income / average equity.*
If we multiply above and below the line by sales revenue and rearrange it, we come up with following formula.

$$ROE= \left\{ \frac{Net\ income}{Sale} \right\} \times \left(\frac{sales}{Average\ equity} \right)$$

And again, by total assets we end up with a formula that looks like this.

$$ROE= \left\{ \frac{Net income}{sale} \right\} \times \left\{ \frac{Sales}{Total\ assets} \right\} \times \left(\frac{Total\ assets}{Average\ equity} \right)$$

The first part net income over sales is the company's net profit margin, the second piece sales over assets is the company's asset turnover and assets over equity is the company's leverage ratio also known as the equity multiplier.

One important thing to realize here is that if we combine these first two parts we end up with net income over assets which is return on assets. Now in terms of interpretation we have looked at these metrics to some extent already.

Net profit margin measures the company's ability to generate profits from their ordinary business activity. A higher number here indicates the company in a good position in their industry.

Asset turnover gives us a measure of how the company is able to generate sales from their assets. This is a valuable comparison mechanism that can be used to compare companies of different sizes. Again, a higher figure indicates a better performing company.

With financial leverage we're looking at the company's financial risk and solvency.

Comparing the company's assets to their equity position is just the same as comparing liabilities plus equity to the equity position. It is a measure of what proportion of the capital structure this company holds on the liability side. Higher number here indicates a company with more obligations, more risk and more chance of insolvency.

DuPont analysis can be extended by further breaking down this first term the net profit margin. For this part we multiply by EBT/EBT and EBIT/EBIT and re arrange to end up with a form that looks like this.

ROE= {Net income/ EBT} x {EBT/ EBIT} x {EBIT/ Sales} x {sales/Average assets} x {Average assets/ average equity}

Now we already know these last two components are asset turnover and the leverage ratio so those are interpreted the same as we had before.

This first term Net income over earnings before tax is known as the tax burden. Earnings before tax over EBIT is also known as the company's interest burden which gives us an indication of how the company's interest expense changes relative to earnings.

The term EBIT over sales is called the EBIT margin. This figure tells us how much the company`s revenues comes from their operating profit, so how much is based on their everyday business activity.

LOS 26e: Calculate and interpret ratios used in equity analysis and credit analysis.

Equity analysis: In equity analysis we evaluate and compare the performance of a company from the perspective of an investor.
The major question is would I include this company in a portfolio.

First of all, we need to be aware of some useful per share quantities.

Basic earnings per share: Income the company has generated for each common share outstanding.
Basic EPS= {Net income - the distributions to preferred shareholders}/ weighted average number of common shares outstanding.
Be careful, EPS in isolation is not the most valuable comparison metric. It heavily dependents on the number of outstanding shares.

Diluted EPS: It is the EPS if all convertible instruments were converted into common stock. There will be an income adjustment needed and the number of common shares will have to change to reflect the conversion.

Cash flow per share = CFO / weighted average number of common shares.

Book value per share =Book value of ordinary equity / weighted average number of common shares.
It tells us, what a common shareholder might get in the event of liquidation.

Now we can use these per share values to calculate valuation ratios.

We are going to look at price to earnings, price to cash flow, and price to book. Each are calculated by taking the price per share and dividing by the relevant per share value we calculated before.

Price to earnings reflects the cost to an investor of partaking in the earnings generated by the company.

Price to cash flow assess the amount that investor has to pay for each dollar of cash flow generated by the company and this metric is useful as an alternative to price earnings and is especially useful in cases where reported earnings are of questionable quality.

Price to book value is the cost paid by an investor per dollar of the company's book value. It's often interpreted as a comparison between the companies expected future return on the return required by the market. If this ratio is greater than one we would expect the company to generate a rate of return in excess of the markets required return.

Dividend related ratios.

The dividend payout ratio = amount of dividend declared/ net income available to common shareholders.

It is a measure of the amount of earnings that are distributed to shareholders.

Retention rate = {net income available to common shareholders -dividend declared}/ net income available to common shareholders

It is a measure of the amount of the company's earnings that were not distributed to shareholders.

Sustainable growth rate = (Retention rate) x (return on equity).

It measures the company's ability to finance their own growth through their ordinary business activities.

Specific ratios

These ratios give us general idea but there are other specific ratios related to specific industry. Financial services companies, for example, are supposed to follow some specific regulations. For these types of companies, ratios like capital adequacy under monetary reserve requirement are important.

In the service industry we might interested in net income per employee or sales per employee ratios.

In the retail industry sales per square foot is important.

Coefficient of variation metrics

We can measure riskiness of different financial statements items like coefficient of variation of sales (CV sales = $\dfrac{Standard\ deviation\ of\ sales}{mean\ sales}$) and CV of net income ($CV\ of\ net\ income = \dfrac{SD\ net\ income}{mean\ net\ income}$) etc.

Credit analysis

Credit analysis is an assessment of the ability of a company to repay their debts. In this we measure credit risk of a company, their credit worthiness and credit risking.

In credit assessment we base our analysis on interest coverage ratio, debt to asset ratio, return on capital ratio cash flow to debt ratio etc. These ratios tell us about the company`s ability to repay debts from core business activities.

LOS26f: Explain the requirements for segment reporting and calculate and interpret segment ratios.

Business segment is a portion of a larger company that accounts for more than ten percent of overall assets or revenues and is distinguishable from the rest of the business.

A company must disclose separate information about any operating entity that meets these criteria.

Although companies are not required to publish financial statements for each of their business segments some amount of segmented reporting is a requirement of both IFRS and U. S. GAAP.

Some of the disclosures that are required for each reportable segment include
- A statement of profit or loss.
- A measure of the assets and liabilities of the segment.
- A report distinguishing between revenue from external customers and revenue from other segments.
- Asset costs and depreciation or amortization expenses.
- Other information related to interest payments interest revenue and tax based on the information disclosed.

And analysts can generate some useful ratios like
- segment margins.
- Assets turned over.
- the segments return on assets.

And with those we can assess the performance of the segment individually to get some more detail on the overall company's performance.

LOS26g: Describe a ratio analysis and other techniques can be used to model and forecast earnings.

If sales revenues forecasts are given analyst can use historic data and trend analysis to forecast certain elements of financial statements like gross profit.

Forecasts are generally a distribution of possible outcomes (and not a single point estimates). In forecast building the techniques like sensitivity analysis, (analysis of changes in inputs), Scenario analysis, Assimilation are used.

Sensitivity analysis: Sensitivity analysis is based on what if conditions. For example, what would happen to gross profit if cost of goods sold changes by 1 percent.

Scenario analysis: Analyzing the effect of a change of a set of input variables.

Assimilation: Taking a distribution of inputs to yield a distribution of outputs.

Inventories Study session 8,

LOS27a: Distinguish between costs included in inventories and costs recognized as expenses in the period in which they are incurred.

In inventory accumulation certain costs are required to be capitalized and other are to be expensed.
The capitalized costs are added into inventory value in balance sheet. These costs are expensed when the inventory is sold.

The expensed costs go into income statement for that period. Note that these would not be part of COGS. These are expenses incurred in the accumulation of inventory that is not being capitalized.

Costs that would be capitalized are called product costs. Product cost = purchase price - discount or rebate+ relevant labor costs + overheads + any other costs incurred in bringing the inventory to its current location in its current condition.

The costs to be expensed are called period costs. This would include any abnormal waste in materials, labor or overheads. Any storage costs that are not required in the production chain any costs of administration and any costs involved in making sales.

LOS27b: Describe different inventory valuation method (Cost formulas).

In this section we are to look for inventory valuation. How do we value the inventory that we have available for sale?

Under IFRS the methodology chosen for valuing inventory is called the cost flow formula. While under U. S. GAAP it is known as the cost flow assumption.
Under IFRS we have three methods for valuing inventory.
- Specific identification
- weighted average
- First in first out.

US GAAP we also have these three methods permitted under IFRS but we are also allowed to use last in first out.
This LOS is all about understanding the difference between the standards and what each of these four methods means.

Specific identification method: Under this method each item in the firm's inventory is matched with its own original cost. When an item is sold accounting for its cost is based on the actual cost of bringing that individual item into the company's inventory. A company that works with a relatively smaller inventory with costly items or very individual or unique items, it is the most appropriate method.
Jewelers for example would use specific identification to account for the cost of their stock.

Weighted average cost method: The weighted average cost method is very simple idea. We takes the total cost of inventory and divide by the number of units available for sale. That gives us the average per unit cost.
We can use that per unit cost to calculate the inventory value by multiplying by the number of units available for sale or we can calculate the cost of goods sold by multiplying by the number of units sold.

First in first out method: The FIFO method. With this method we assume that the oldest item in inventory is sold first. We sell items in the order that they were brought into stock. But this has two major effects for the financial statements.

1. Because the oldest items are the ones being sold the cost of goods sold will be based on some potentially much older stock. This means potentially much older pricing.
2. Because the items remaining in inventory are newer stock which were purchased more recently its value may be closer to the current market value so in essence what we're going to get is a cost of goods sold figure which might be out of date.

Last in first out LIFO method: This is opposite to FIFO method. When the inventory is sold it is the most recently purchased items that are sold first. The effect of this is that now the cost of goods sold figure will more accurately reflect current market prices while inventory valuation will be based on some potentially older prices. So, we have a more accurate cost of goods sold and a potentially out of date inventory evaluation.

LOS27c: Calculate and compare cost of sales, Gross profit, and ending inventory using different inventory valuation methods and using perpetual and periodic inventory systems.

In this LOS we need to go through these inventory valuation methods and to calculate cost of sales and ending inventory in each case. Then we will go through periodic and perpetual inventory systems.

Let's say for example, a company has 200 units in stock at the beginning of the period with the per unit cost of 2$. During the period they have one order for 100 units at 2.5$ and a second order of 150 more units at a per unit cost 3$.

We're going to calculate the cost of goods sold and inventory value at the period end using the three methods.

Assuming that a total of 400 units were sold during the period leaving 50 units remaining.

Weighted average method: With the weighted average method the first task is to calculate the weighted average cost per unit.

$$Weighted\ average\ cost\ of\ inventory = \frac{\sum_{1}^{n} XiPi}{total\ units\ purchased} = \frac{400 + 250 + 450}{200 + 100 + 150} = 2.44\$$$

Where x is the number of units purchased and p is the price. We multiply number of units purchased with their price and sum up. Then we divide this sum by total units purchased the result would be our weighted average cost of each unit purchased.

Opening inventory	200 units @2 $	400 $
Purchased	100 @ 2.5$	250$
Purchased	150 @ 3$	450$
Cost of goods available for sale	(200 +100 + 150) * 2.44 = 1098	
Ending inventory	50 * 2.44 = 122	
Cost of goods sold	1098 – 122 = 976	

Lets say we have total sales revenues are 1500$ then our gross profit will be 1500 – 976= 524$.

FIFO: With the first in first out method we sold the units from the oldest boxes in stock first even when we had newer boxes available.

That means first we sold 200 units that were purchased at s$/ unit. Then we sold 100 units who were purchased at 2.5$/unit. Lastly, we sold 100 units of 3$/unit. So we are left with 50 units bought at 3$. So the calculation is as follows.

Opening inventory	200 units @2 $	400 $	Sold 200 units of 2$
Purchased	100 @ 2.5$	250 $	Sold 100 units of 2.5$
Purchased	150 @ 3$	450 $	Sold 100 units of 3$
Cost of goods available for sale	(400 +250 + 450) = 1100		
Ending inventory	50 *3 = 150$		
Cost of goods sold	1100 – 150 = 950		

Lets say we have total sales revenues are 1500$ then our gross profit will be 1500 – 950= 550$.

LIFO: Last in first out: The last in first out method is only allowed under U. S. GAAP. It is not permitted under IFRS.

Opening inventory	200 units @2 $	400 $	Sold 200 units of 2$
Purchased	100 @ 2.5$	250 $	
Purchased	150 @ 3$	450 $	
Cost of goods available for sale	(400 +250 + 450) = 1100		
Ending inventory	50 *2 = 100$		

Cost of goods sold	1100 – 100 = 1000$		

Lets say we have total sales revenues are 1500$ then our gross profit will be 1500 – 1000= 500$.

When we compare these three methods in terms of their effect on gross profit we need to look at the cost of goods sold figure side by side while considering the pattern of the purchase price.

No, we are not given specific information on the dates of the orders here so we can't really paint an accurate picture of the price trend but we can at least have gathered that the prices are increasing.

With rising prices FIFO produces the lowest cost of goods sold figure.

Weighted average is in average while LIFO produces the highest.

Now given that gross profit is given by taking the cost of goods sold away from net sales revenue. This will mean that again under rising prices.

FIFO will produce the highest gross profit, LIFO for the lowest with weighted average somewhere in between.

Perpetual and periodic systems are the two most common ways that a company will record changes in inventory.

Perpetual system: In this method inventory and cost of goods sold are continuously updated.

Sale and purchase transactions are recorded directly in inventory and cost of goods sold so there's no need for a purchases account.

Periodic inventory system: The values of inventory and cost of goods sold are determined at the end of an accounting period. No detailed account is maintained. The inventory purchased during a year is reported in purchases account. At the end of each period purchases are added into opening inventory to determine cost of goods sold.

Let's take a look at an example of how this works. Here we have some purchases and sales data for a company's first quarter of business.

Purchases	5000	3.5$per unit
sales	2100	7 $ /unit
sales	1700	7 $ /unit
purchases	5000	4.5$ /unit
sales	1500	7$ /unit
sales	1800	7$ /unit

We're going to assume that they had no inventory on hand at the beginning of the period. We are going to analyze the effect of choosing between the perpetual and periodic inventory system.

To perform this analysis, step one is to calculate sales revenue. This is going to be the same under both methods. Step two then is to calculate ending inventory. Step three is to use ending inventory to calculate cost of goods sold. And finally, then step for is to use sales revenue and cost of goods sold to get gross profit.

1. sales revenue. Add all the sold units. It will be 7100 units. Each of these units were sold for seven dollars so the company's total sales revenue =7100 x 7 =49700$.
Next let's go through steps two three and four using the perpetual system and the LIFO method.
2.To calculate the value of closing inventory we need to figure out the makeup of inventories as it exists at the end of the period.

units	Per unit	Available units
5000	3.5$	5000@3.5
-2100		(5000-2100 =) 2900 @3.5
-1700		(2900- 1700)= 1200@3.5
5000	4.5$	1200 @ 3.5 and 5000 @4.5
-1500		1200 @3.5 and 3500@4.5
-1800		1200 @3.5 and 1700 @4.5

Working through the purchase and sale transactions. We find that this company ends up with 1200 units at the 3.5 price level and a 1700 units at 4.5 price level.
So, the total value of ending inventory is = (1200x3.5) + (1700x4.5) =11850$

The next step is to calculate the cost of goods sold. To do that we first need to calculate the total cost of purchased goods.
This is simply a case of pulling out the purchase transactions, multiplying the number of units by the price per unit and taking a total.

Here we have a total cost of purchase = (5000x3.5) +(5000x4.5) =40000$
So, cost of goods sold = cost of purchase - value of ending inventory = 40000 - 11850= 28150$

Last step then is to calculate gross profit for the perpetual system.
Gross profit = Sales revenues- cost of goods sold= 49700-28150= 21550$

Periodic method with LIFO: Since we know that sales revenue is the same as before we can go straight to step 2 the value of ending inventory. This system is a bit different. All we need to do here is go through the purchase and sale transactions to find out how many units are remaining at the end of the period. We then apply the cost price of the oldest purchase transaction as the value for all remaining units.

Now our ending units are 5000 -2100 -1700 +5000 -1500 -1800 = 2900 which costs 3.5@ (the oldest are remained with oldest cost.) So, the cost of ending inventory is 2900 x 3.5 =10150.
Now if we had more than 5000 units in closing inventory then we wouldn't be able to use that price of 3.5 on its own because only 5000 units were ever available at that price.

{For example, if we had 6000 units remaining we would take 5000 units at the price of 3.5$ the oldest price and the other 1000 units would be taking out a cost level from the next oldest price level of 4.5$ in line with the last in first principle.}

Following on that we need to calculate the cost of goods sold. With the periodic system we work our way through the sales data using the most recent cost price of 4.5$ until we have accounted for 500 units.
After that we move on to the older 3.5$ price.
In this case we have 5000 units which will be accounted for using the newer 4.5 price and 2100 units which will be accounted for using the older 3.5 price.

So, COGS= (5000x 4.5) x 2100x3.5= 29850$.
And, Gross profit = Sales-COGS= 49700-29850=19850

How these figures compare side by side using the two methods.

	Perpetual	Periodic
Sales	49700	49700
Ending inventory	11850	10150
COGS	28150	29850
Gross profit	21550	19850

LOS 27.d: Calculate and explain how inflation and deflation of inventory costs affect the financial statements and ratios of companies that use different inventory valuation methods.

When prices are rising (inflation) LIFO will give us higher cost of goods sold and lower value of inventory in hand. It's because most recent units are sold first which are costly than older units. It means less gross profit and net profit will be reported in income statement.

With increasing prices FIFO will give us lower cost of goods sold but higher inventory in hand. This is because of the older units with cheaper prices are sold first while the newer units (with higher prices) will be kept in stock. It means we would be having higher gross and net profits than LIFO method.

When prices are falling (deflation) the pattern will be other way around. In this situation LIFO gives us less cost of goods sold and higher inventory in hand while higher gross and net profits.
FIFO will give us higher COGS, lower inventory in hand, lower gross and net profits.
Also, with rising prices LIFO gives us lower tax expense as COGS would be higher.

LOS 27.e: Explain LIFO reserve and LIFO liquidation and their effects on financial statements and ratios.
LOS 27.f: Convert a company's reported financial statements from LIFO to FIFO for purposes of comparison.

We know that ending inventory value is lower under LIFO than FIFO. When a company reports under LIFO, they are required to report LIFO reserve.

LIFO reserve is the amount by which LIFO inventory is lower than FIFO inventory. This reserve is maintained to allow ease of comparison among companies using LIFO and FIFO.
To compare financial statement prepared under LIFO with those prepared under FIFO an analyst must
- Add LIFO reserve to LIFO inventory on the balance sheet
- Add LIFO reserve in retained earnings

There is another problem here. When LIFO is used in rising prices, company has lower earnings so lower the tax paid. SO, the company has more cash and retained earnings must also be adjusted accordingly. So, analyst must minus LIFO reserve x tax rate from cash (on balance sheet). And retained earnings are also increased by LIFO reserve (1-tax rate) instead of full LIFO reserve.

For comparison analyst must also convert LIFO COGS into FIFO COGS. The difference between LIFO COGS and FIFO COGS is change in LIFO reserve account. So, FIFO COGS= LIFO COGS – {LIFO reserve at end of period -LIFO reserve at beginning period}.

case of falling prices the difference between LIFO ending and beginning amount would be negative. In this case this will be added into LIFO COGS to convert it into FIFO COGS.

> **Challenge Question:** ABC limited is using LIFO method of inventory. They reported ending inventory of 5m$ in 2xx7 and of 4 m $ in 2xx8. COGS for the year 2xx8 are 10m$. LIFO reserve was 0.5 m in 2xx7 and 0.8m in 2xx8. Convert inventory and COGS of 2xx8 from LIFO to FIFO.

Effects on Ratios

We assume increase in prices while looking at the effects of adjustments from LIFO to FIFO on ratios.

Profitability ratios: LIFO produces higher COGS than FIFO and lower earnings. So, conversion from LIFO to FIFO gives us higher profitability ratios. For example, higher gross, operating, and net profit margins as compared to LIFO.

Liquidity: In comparison to FIFO, LIFO gives us lower inventory value on the balance sheet because inventory is higher under FIFO. **The current ratio** is also higher under FIFO (because current assets are higher). Working capital is also higher under FIFO (working capital = current assets – current liabilities, and current assets are higher).

The quick ratio is unaffected by the firm's chosen inventory method because inventory is excluded from its numerator.

Activity ratios: we know that COGS are higher and inventory is lower under LIFO so Inventory turnover (COGS / average inventory) is also higher than FIFO. So, when we convert it from LIFO to FIFO we got lower inventory turnover ratio. When we got lower inventory turnover it means higher days of inventory in hand as (365 / inventory turnover).

Solvency ratios: LIFO gives us lower total assets (because inventory is lower) than FIFO so, when we convert form LIFO to FIFO we got higher total assets and higher stockholders' equity (assets – liabilities).

Because total assets and stockholders' equity are higher under FIFO, debt-to-equity ratio is lower under FIFO.

LOS27g: Describe the measurement of inventory at the lower of cost or net realizable value.

In this section we are to look at the measurement of inventory value under IFRS and U. S. GAAP

Under IFRS *we must value inventory at the lower of cost or net realizable value.*
Net realizable value = expected sales price - completion costs - selling costs.
If cost is lower than net realizable value then it must be recorded at cost. And if subsequently net realizable value falls below cost the value of inventory must then be written down to account for that loss in value. And that loss would have to be reflected on the income statement.
After written down if realizable value subsequently increases again. IFRS allows us to reverse the original right down that took us from the original cost level down to the lower net realizable value level. So, we post an increase to the inventory account and the gain to the income statement. It is known as a reversal of a right down.
These transactions would generally occur in a contra account called a valuation allowance account so that changes in value are kept separate from initial cost.

Under US GAAP inventory is valued at the lower of cost or market.
Market value = replacement cost, (but cannot be greater than Net realizable value). or
Market value < NRV - normal profit margin.
If replacement cost >NRV, then market is net realizable value. If replacement cost is , NRV - normal profit margin, then market is NRV -normal profit margin.
Again, in this case where current market value was below the reported valuation of inventory a write down is performed and a loss is recognized on the income statement.

But U. S. GAAP does not allow write ups or reversals in the case of a subsequent increase in value.

One interesting point to note is that because firms reporting inventory levels based on the LIFO method will have their inventory value based on older and likely lower cost levels. They will be less likely to experience a right down.

LOS 27.h: Describe implications of valuing inventory at net realizable value for financial statements and ratios.

When we write down inventory to net realizable value it affects financial statements in many ways as follows
- Inventory is included in current assets, a written in inventory will decrease in current assets and also in total assets.

- A decrease in total assets causes increase in total asset turnover (**Sales / Average Total Assets) and debt to assets ratio.**
- Inventory turnover (COGS/ Average inventory) increases but days inventory in hand and cash conversion cycle decreases.
- Shareholder`s equity decreased so the debt to equity ratio increases.
- Due to increase in COGS gross profit margin, operating profit margin and net profit margin decreases.
- Percentage decrease in net income is often more than percentage decrease in assets and or equity. So, return on assets and return on equity decreases.
- The current ratio (current assets/ current liabilities) decreases. Not effect on quick ratio as we do not include inventory in it.
- In subsequent years of written down COGS may be decrease as we have lower inventory value so the profit margins will increase and so the ROA and ROE.

LOS27i: Describe the financial statement presentation of and disclosures relating to inventories.

Disclosures related to inventory

Under IFRS and US GAAP companies are required to disclose the following
- Accounting policies followed related to measurement. (It means the valuation method and cost flow formula).
- Carrying value by classification. (That means a breakdown of inventory value split out into raw materials, production supplies, works in progress and finished units ready for sale).
- The value of units held at fair value less selling costs.
- The cost of goods sold or cost of sales.
- Any write downs recognize in the period.
- Any reversals of write downs recognize in the period.
- The circumstances leading to write downs or reversals (GAAP does not allow reversal).
- Any inventory pledged as collateral against liabilities.

Changes in inventory
A firm can change inventory cost flow methods normally retrospectively (the previous year's financial statements are restated using new cost flow method). An exception to retrospective application is when a firm change *to LIFO* from another cost flow method. In this case, the change is applied prospectively; no adjustments are made to the prior periods.

Under IFRS, the firm must explain that the change will provide reliable and more relevant information. Under U.S. GAAP, the firm must explain why the change in inventory method is preferable.

LOS 27.j: Explain issues that analysts should consider when examining a company's inventory disclosures and other sources of information.

Some firms, like wholesaler and retailers (also called merchandising firms), do not manufacture goods. They only buy and sell. Their goods are ready to sale. So, they record inventory in one account only in the balance sheet.

Other firms who manufacture goods record goods in usually three accounts, raw material, work in process and finished goods.

An analyst must use this information about inventory along with management discussion and analysis, industry reports and other data to determine about future revenues of the firm.

Let's say a firm has more inventory in hand. It can be related to increase in demand so the firm is collecting more inventory. If sales are reduced with an increase in inventory and finished goods. It can be described as reduction in demand and inventory can be getting obsolete and there is a risk of inventory write down.
Higher inventory turnover is good but if it is combined with low sales growth, it means firm is not holding adequate inventory which can cause a further reduction in sales.

High inventory turnover may also mean that an inventory write-down has occurred which is a sign of poor inventory management. But higher sale growth with higher inventory turnover may reflect efficiency.

LOS 27.k: Calculate and compare ratios of companies, including companies that use different inventory methods.
LOS 27.l: Analyze and compare the financial statements of companies, including companies that use different inventory methods.

In these LOS we have to compare ratios and financial statements of companies using different inventory methods. It is very mush discussed in the whole inventory section. A quick review is as follows:

Here we're going to be focusing on the effect of the choice between them when it comes to ratios.

You remember that using weighted average cost method will land figures like cost of goods sold an inventory value somewhere in between LIFO and FIFO.

Inventory management is all about balance.

Too much inventory brings about costs like storage obsolescence or insurance. Too little inventory brings about the potential cost of experiencing a stock shortage and missing out on a sale.

We have two major ratios to look at when assessing a company's inventory management.
Inventory turnover and days inventory in hand.
You will remember these ratios from earlier in the material. Inventory turnover = COGS/average inventory.
Days inventory on hand = 365/ inventory turnover.
From the formula for each we can figure out why the inventory valuation method is important.

We know that the denominator of inventory turnover formula is average inventory. With a change in method of inventory valuation, we will experience change in average inventory and that would affect the ratios.

When we consider inventory in management by ratio analysis we need to be aware of the inventory valuation method as well as the underlying business to build a meaningful comparison or evaluation.

One important factor for assessment is that these ratios have an inverse relationship.
High inventory return over means a low number of days in inventory on hand.
Low days inventory on hand means that the company doesn't have units in its inventory for long before they are sold that sounds great as soon as they get stocking ready for sale it's gone.

Now on the other hand this might mean that the company doesn't hold enough inventory compared to what sales demand would deem appropriate or it might mean that they have recently experienced an inventory right down.

There are a number of possibilities as to what it means to have a low number of days inventory on hand.
One of the ratio which is directly affected by the choice of inventory evaluation method is the gross profit margin.

Gross profit margin is given by gross profit over revenue and since gross profit is equal to sales revenue minus cost of goods sold, a choice affecting cost of goods sold will indirectly impact gross profit and also gross profit margin.

Long lived assets Study session 8

LOS 28a: Distinguish between costs that are capitalized and costs that are expensed in the period in which they are incurred.

In long lived assets we have tangibles like plant and machinery, building, tools etc. and intangible assets like good will, patent etc.

In this section we need to distinguish between the costs which are capitalized and costs which are expensed related to acquiring long lived assets.

The basic rule is simple. Any expenditure that is expected to provide a future economic benefit over multiple periods must be capitalized. Capitalized costs are recorded in balance sheet at purchasing price or fair value.

When an expenditure is not expected to provide a future economic benefit over multiple periods it should be expensed in the current period. These are recorded on the income statement and being counted with operating cash flows.

There are various types of cost they're expected to provide multiple years of economic benefit. For example, if a major part of the machine is replaced. The cost of that part should be capitalized because it would be expected to provide the multiple years of economic benefit.

Anything that extends the useful life of an asset should be capitalized.

On the other hand, training costs or costs for regular maintenance would be examples of costs that will not provide multiple periods of economic benefit. These kinds of costs must be expensed in the current period and you will be expected to be able to discern between these types of costs and understand which should be capitalized and which should be expensed.

LOS28b: Compare the financial reporting of the following types of intangible assets: Purchased, internally developed, acquired in a business combination.

Intangible assets are assets that do not bear a physical substance.

They are of two types.   Identifiable assets.   And   unidentifiable assets.

Identifiable intangible: These are assets that represent a contractual or legal right that can be separated from the owning entity under expected to generate a future economic benefit.
These assets might include.
- Patents.
- Copyrights.
- Brand recognition or a trademark.

An unidentifiable intangible asset an asset that bears no physical substance and it does not match the criteria of identifiable intangible assets.
One good example of unidentifiable intangible asset is good will, the excessive purchase price over the fair value of assets acquired.

There are two other broad categories of intangible asset.
- Assets with finite lives
- Assets with indefinite life

Asset with a finite life must be amortized (Similar to a tangible asset). Whereas the cost of an asset with an indefinite life will not be amortized but will be tested annually for impairment.
If impairment occurs then the assets value will be written down on the balance sheet and the firm report a loss on their income statement.
Accounting for intangibles depends on how they were acquired.
- Assets might be purchased.
- Developed internally.
- Or acquired as part of the business combination.

When an asset is purchased, the accounting treatment is quite similar to tangible long lived assets.
The purchase price is assumed to be equal to fair value and that's the figure used to record the asset on the balance sheet. Then
For assets that were developed internally the accounting treatment is a bit different.

When an asset is purchased the company will have one easily identifiable transaction that can drive an asset being capitalized on the balance sheet.

Assets which are developed internally will have come about through a series of expenses the company would have recognized in the periods which they were incurred. The company will have spent money over time on a wide variety of expenses and it's the combination of all of these varying expenses that lead the company to own this intangible asset. So, the company will recognize a series of expenditures on their income statement over time. These together will develop into an intangible asset that they own.

A good example would be continuous expenditures on R & D program or an advertising or marketing plan.

Over time these might develop into a recognizable brand and brand recognition.

The differing accounting treatments we have seen here will spark a major difference between the financial statements of companies who purchase assets and those who have developed them internally.

On the one hand you have companies with assets on the balance sheet compared to companies that do not have assets to report. This is because companies who develop their assets internally will had expense their acquisition costs as they were being developed.

At the same time, you have these purchasing companies recognizing expenditures as investing cash flows. While the companies developing the assets are recognizing these expenses as operating cash flows.

Intangibles acquired as part of the business combination: Assets acquired through a business combination are accounted for using the acquisition methods. Assets acquired are recorded on the balance sheet of the acquirer at fair value. The difference between the overall purchase price and the combined amount attributable to the acquired assets is recorded as good will.

It's important to know that this is what we consider good will to be an on identifiable intangible asset. It cannot be separated from the acquired business.

LOS 28.c: Explain and evaluate how capitalizing versus expensing costs in the period in which they are incurred affects financial statements and ratios.

When the cost is capitalized or expensed the choice affects net income, shareholders' equity, total assets, cash flow from operations, cash flow from investing and financial ratios. Let`s see how it affect

Net income:
When a firm chooses to capitalize expenditure, it postpones the recognition of an expense in the income statement. So, the firm will report higher net income. But in coming years, when the capitalized expense is reported in the income statement in the process of amortization or depreciation firm will report lower net income.

However, the total net income remains same under both the techniques over the life time of asset. Since both capitalizing and expensing have different effects on the financial statements, an analyst should adjust the numbers for a better comparison.

Shareholders' Equity
We know that capitalization gives us higher net income, it also increases higher shareholders' equity as retained earnings are greater. As capitalizing results in asset creation so total assets increased but liabilities are unaffected. When the cost is to be allocated to the income statement in coming years, net income, retained earnings, and shareholders' equity will be reduced.

If firm chooses to expense, retained earnings and shareholders' equity will be decreased in those periods.

Cash Flow statement: When we capitalize expenditure is goes into cash flow statement under cash flow from investing activities as outflow. One the other hand if the expenditure is expenses it goes into cash flow from operations as outflow. It means capitalizing gives us higher cash flow from operations and less cash flow from investing activities. And expensing an expenditure gives us lower cash flow from operations and higher cash flow from investing activities. If we assume there is no tax difference the total of cash flow statement remains same.

Financial Ratios: when we capitalize an expenditure, we are actually increasing total assets and equity (in current period). So, the ratios in which total assets or equity are in denominator, like debt to asset and debt to equity are lower. And off course ratios with total assets or equity in nominator are higher like ROA, ROE. In subsequent periods the ROA ROE will be lower as we have to depreciate the capitalized expense.

When a firm recognizes an expenditure as expense, in the first period net income, Total assets and equity will decrease. So, the ratios like ROE and ROA will be lower. In subsequent periods these ratios will be higher. An analyst must be very careful in judging firms.

If a firm buys an asset with a loan and pays interest. Firm can capitalize that interest expenditure. By capitalizing interest expenditure, the total interest expense goes down. So, the interest coverage ratio (EBIT/interest expense) which measures firm`s ability to meet interest expense, will be higher (which is a good sign). So, a firm who decided to expense interest expenditure comes up with lower interest coverage ratio. Analyst must calculate interest coverage ratio by using total interest expenditure (including capitalized interest). So, this is considered to be a better measure and bond rating companies often use this method.

LOS 28d: Describe the different depreciation methods for property, plant and equipment, calculate depreciation expense.

LOS 28e: Describe how the choice of depreciation method and assumptions concerning useful life and residual value affect depreciation expense, financial statements, and ratios.

Different depreciation methods for property plant and equipment.
We have three methods.
- Straight line
- Accelerated
- Units of production.

Straight-line method: In this method we allocate an equal amount of the asset`s value to each year of its depreciable life (useful life).

We take the cost of the asset minus salvage value and divide by the number of years. Formula

Depreciation per year = {Cost of asset- salvage value}/ number of useful years

Accelerated method: It is used when a greater proportion of the asset`s cost is allocated to the earlier years of its useful life. This method is more appropriate in cases where the actual usage of the asset is greater in its earlier years.

One commonly used accelerated depreciation method is the <u>double declining balance method.</u>

Under this system two things can change compared to the straight-line method.

First, we use an acceleration factor of two on the left to increase the proportion of the assets valued appreciated in the early years.

And second instead of handling the salvage value here in the calculation of the expense amount we account for the accumulated depreciation as we progress through time. We will handle salvage value by stopping the depreciation process when the asset`s carrying value, (historical cost less accumulated depreciation) reaches that salvage value. The formula is as under

Depreciation for a period = 2 x straight-line

Units of production method: In this system the assets value is allocated based on the actual usage of the asset in a particular period rather than trying to model the usage of the asset over its useful life.

When we model the usage of the asset over its useful life, a company will be paying much closer attention to the actual usage of the asset and depreciation is based on a much closer reflection of reality.

$$\text{Depreciation for a year} = \frac{cost - salvage\ value}{life\ ife\ in\ output\ units} * output\ units\ in\ that\ period$$

Component depreciation: IFRS requires the depreciation of an asset in components. For example, building has components of walls. Roof etc. and furniture has tables, chairs etc. each of these components is depreciated separately. In US GAAP we do not use component depreciation

Effects: Now we need to describe the effect of the choice of depreciation method on the financial statements and ratios.

The choice of depreciation method affects the company's reported assets through changes in the asset`s carrying values. They are affecting operating income through the amount of the depreciation expense and their net income through the depreciation expense.

This in turn will affect any ratios that use those figures like

Fixed asset turnover, Total asset turnover, operating profit margin, operating return on assets and return on assets.

Now from the formula for the straight-line method we can see that the depreciation expense is inversely related to both useful life and salvage value.

If the company assumes a longer useful life then the depreciation expense comes down. And if the company assumes a higher salvage value depreciation expense comes down.

For this section we need to be aware of the fact that companies will sometimes use the useful life and residual value of an asset to manipulate a depreciation schedule and an indirect came of that is to manipulate earnings.

Remember that longer useful lives and higher residual values bring down the depreciation expense which will mean a higher income.

Calculation of depreciation has been covered in reading on expense recognition on the income statement.

LOS 28f: Describe the different amortization methods for intangible assets with finite lives, and calculate amortization expense.

LOS 28g: Describe how the choice of amortization method and assumptions concerning useful life and residual value affect amortization expense, financial statements, and ratios.

Here we are only considering intangibles with finite lives here. We're not going to test goodwill for impairment right now.

When we are calculating amortization for intangibles that have finite lives. The methods (of amortization) are exactly the same as depreciation of tangible assets.

Straight line, accelerated and units of production. It's all about allocating the cost of the asset to the years of its useful life.

Calculation of amortization expense
Let`s say a company A acquired another company and now they report some intangible assets on their book as follows.

Intangible asset	value	Useful life.
Patent	$800000	5 years
Copyright	$300000	10 (with $10000 residual value)
Good will	$100000	

Using the straight-line method calculate the total carrying value of company`s intangible assets at the end of the year.

We know that straight line amortization (also depreciation) formula.

$$Amortization\ expense\ for\ each\ year = \frac{(Cost - salvage\ or\ residual\ value)}{useful\ life.}$$

For patent we have a cost of 800000 and 5 years useful life and we have not been given a residual value so plugging that information into the formula we get

$$\frac{(800000 - 0)}{5} = 160000$$

With copyright we have a cost of 300000 and 10-year useful life and a residual value of 10000. Again, plugging into the formula, we come up with an amortization expense

$$\frac{(300000 - 10000)}{10} = 29000$$

Remember that goodwill is an intangible asset with indefinite useful life so there won't be any amortization charge. We only amortize intangible assets that have finite useful lives.

Intangible asset	value	Amortization expense
Patent	$800000	160000
Copyright	$300000	29000
Good will	$100000	0
Total amortization expense for the period		189000
Intangibles at end of period	800000+300000+100000 -189000 =1011000	

The effect of the choice of amortization method on the financial statements:
Through changes in carrying values and amortization expenses the company will see an impact on assets, income and ratios depending on their choice regarding the method of amortization chosen.

Describe the effects of assumptions concerning useful life and residual value on amortization expense.
Again, important point here is that the inverse relationship exists between the expense and useful life and residual value. Longer lives means higher residual values would equate to the company recognizing a lower amortization expense in the period.

LOS 28h: Describe the revaluation model.

The revaluation model is a simple system, rarely used in practice, for reporting the value of a firm's assets. This is only allowed under IFRS. Under U. S. GAAP companies must report their balance sheet assets using the historical cost model.

This model is opposite to the historical cost model. (In historical cost model we report original cost minus accumulated depreciation amount on the balance sheet along with the depreciation expense on the income statement), In revaluation model we report the assets on the balance sheet at fair value and post a gradual decline in fair value as losses to the income statement.

Following are the condition must be fulfilled in order to use this model

- An active market must exist for the asset. Without an active market in place reliable estimates of fair value would be impossible to obtain.
- Firms must be using similar methods of reporting for similar assets. It means they cannot pick and choose certain assets to report under the historical cost model and then others to report using the revaluation model.
- Assets are written down in value with usage and age as the fair value declines. As the asset`s value in the active market changes so should the reported value change.

Note: if the value of the asset increases in the market and that increase goes beyond the asset`s initial cost, that gain should be reported as a revaluation surplus with shareholders equity and not as a gain on the income statement.

LOS 28i: Explain the impairment of property plant and equipment and intangible assets.

Depreciation and amortization are scheduled models for the decline in assets value over its useful life, impairment is reserved for a decline in the assets value at a particular point in time which was not anticipated.

The first major point we need to make here is that a company will only test the value of an asset for impairment if there is an indication that an impairment may have occurred (may be due to some incident like obsolescence, A decline in demand or maybe a technological advancement).
Remember that we need a reason to test for impairment.

Under IFRS testing for impairment means looking at the difference between asset`s carrying value and its recoverable value.

Carrying value = asset`s original cost - accumulated depreciation - any previous impairments or reversals. It is the currently reported value of the asset.

Recoverable value is either the asset`s fair value less any costs that would have to be incurred to Sell it or the asset`s value in use, whichever is higher.

Value in use is the present value of the asset`s expected future cash flows if usage continued.

So, under IFRS we have an impaired asset if the carrying value is greater than the recoverable value. When that occurs, the company must write down or decrease the value of the asset as recorded on their balance sheet. And they would record a loss equal to that change in value on their income statement.
Note that an impairment loss is a non-cash amount so the cash flow statement will not see any impact.

Under U. S. GAAP we impair an asset if carrying value is greater than fair value.
It means the company will only write down the asset`s value and post a loss to the income statement if the assets carrying value is deemed to be not recoverable. So even if fair value is actually less than the asset`s current carrying value, a write down will only be recorded if the asset`s carrying value is also below the sum of its expected future cash flows.

This isn't the same thing as value in use from IFRS. Value in use is an IFRS measure.
With US GAAP we're comparing carrying value to both fair value and the undiscounted sum of the asset`s expected future cash flows.

Following the write down if an asset's value increases companies reporting with IFRS may report an impairment reversal. They can increase the value of the asset on their reports to reflect that increase in value even after they have posted a loss for a prior decline in value.
U. S. GAAP does not allow for impairment reversals.

LOS28j: Explain the de-recognition of property plant and equipment and intangible assets.

Derecognition is the process by which a company removes an asset from its financial statements.
There are three situations whereby an asset will be de recognized.
- When the asset is sold.
- Exchanged.
- Or abandoned.

When an asset is sold the difference between the sale proceeds in the assets carrying value will go into income statement either as a gain or as a loss. That same figure will also need to be recognized on the cash flow statement as an investing cash inflow.

If an old asset is exchanged for a newer one we will be removing the carrying value of the old asset from the balance sheet and adding the fair value of the new asset as well as that a gain or loss will hit the income statement to reflect the difference between the fair value of the new asset and the carrying value of the old asset.

If an asset is abandoned or retired. The treatment is very similar to a sale only in this case there will be no sale proceeds. There will be a loss to the income statement and since no cash changes hands the cash flow statement will not be affected.

LOS 28.k: Explain and evaluate how impairment, revaluation, and derecognition of property, plant, and equipment and intangible assets affect financial statements and ratios.

Impairment: Impairment reduces the value of asset (tangible and intangible). We record it as loss in income statement, reduce it from retained earnings (equity) and asset. So, the Return on assets (ROA) and Return on equity (ROE) ratios are lower as net income declined. In coming years, as we have impaired the asset`s value, the depreciation expense will be less. So, the net income would be higher (than that if the asset was not impaired) so does the ROA and ROE. Asset turnover ratio would be higher in impairment year and subsequent years as asset`s value is lower now. As the impairment is a non-cash loss, there would be no effect on cash flow statement.

Analysis of impairment: when company impairs its assets, that means the management failed to depreciate or amortize the asset according to the market conditions. It also means that they were recognizing less expense and more income in previous years. Recognition of impairment can be a good opportunity for management to manipulate earnings and ROE, ROA etc. sometimes management decides not to recognize the impairment loss until the year of good earnings to show smooth income pattern. On the other hand, early impairment loss could be done by management to show higher income and ROE, ROA in coming years. A good level of judgment from analyst is required to understand the reason behind the impairment.

Revaluation: US GAAP mostly does not allow revaluation. We only record long lived assets as cost minus depreciation less any impairment. One exception to this rule is for long lived assets held for sale. In this case the previous impairment can be reversed.

Under IFRS we can use revaluation method and can reverse impairment. IFRS allows us to use revaluation model for some assets and cost model for others.

Revaluation has following affects:

- It increases asset`s value so the equity increases.
- It lower leverage ratios i.e. debt to total assets and debt to total equity (as denominator increases).
- When asset`s value increases then the depreciation expense also increases (as we calculate depreciation as percentage of asset`s value). So, the net income decreases.
- ROA and ROE decreases as numerator decreases and denominator increases.

Analysis for revaluation: Analyst must check the reason behind the revaluation because it can also be a good opportunity for management to manipulate results. He/ she must look for industry overview and market conditions for asset`s value.

Derecognition of Assets: Derecognition is the process by which a company removes an asset from its financial statements.

There are three situations whereby an asset will be de recognized.

- When the asset is sold.
- Exchanged.
- Or abandoned.

When an asset is sold the difference between the sale proceeds in the assets carrying value will go into income statement either as a gain or as a loss. That same figure will also need to be recognized on the cash flow statement as an investing cash inflow.

If an old asset is exchanged for a newer one we will be removing the carrying value of the old asset from the balance sheet and adding the fair value of the new asset as well as that a gain or loss will hit the income statement to reflect the difference between the fair value of the new asset and the carrying value of the old asset.

If an asset is abandoned or retired. The treatment is very similar to a sale only in this case there will be no sale proceeds. There will be a loss to the income statement and since no cash changes hands the cash flow statement will not be affected.

LOS28I: Describe the financial statement presentation of and disclosures relating to property plant and equipment, and intangible assets.

For companies reporting under IFRS each of the following items must be disclosed for property plant and equipment.
- The basis for measuring the asset`s value (i.e. historical cost etc.),
- Depreciation method and depreciation rate used,
- Gross carrying value of asset, a reconciliation of any change in the asset`s carrying value over the period,
- Any restrictions related to the asset`s that are pledged as collateral and any agreements which you're currently in place for the future acquisition of assets.

For intangible assets, all above disclosures plus a disclosure of whether the intangible asset`s useful life is finite or indefinite, is required.

For impaired assets we need to disclose
- The amounts of any impairment write downs or reversals.
- Impacts of those write downs and reversals on the income statement
- Circumstances that brought about that impairment or reversal.

For investment property disclosures depend on the valuation method used. We will discuss then later on but in terms of disclosures firms that report under the cost model would follow the same guidelines as ordinary long-lived assets. Firms reporting using the fair value model will be required to include additional disclosures related to the determination of fair value.

Under U. S. GAAP the disclosure requirements are not as detailed. Companies must disclose the aggregate depreciation expense for the period, classified carrying values of the major depreciable asset classes and a general description of the depreciation method used.

For intangible assets a company will have similar disclosure requirements like, aggregate amortization expense amount, Classified listing of growth carrying amounts, Classified accumulated amortization figures, And the estimate for the expected amortization expense for the next five years.

Companies reporting under U. S. GAAP do not have the option of reversing impairments.

For impaired assets, following disclosures are required under U. S. GAAP
- a description of the impaired assets,
- the circumstances that led to the impairment,

- the method used to determine the asset's fair value,
- the amount of the impairment loss and what the impact it has on the income statement.

LOS 28.m: Analyze and interpret financial statement disclosures regarding property, plant, and equipment and intangible assets.

Financial statement disclosures regarding property plant and equipment are helpful for an analyst to understand company's fixed assets and choice of depreciation and or amortization taken. One most common metric used by analyst form this information is to calculate average age of an asset. Average age calculation has two benefits:
- The average useful life gives us the timings of future capital expenditure and financing requirement of the firm.
- To estimate if the older asset might be giving the owning entity a comparative disadvantage.

Following are some useful calculations for analyst:

Average age of assets in years $= \dfrac{Accumulated\ depreciation}{current\ year\ depreciation\ expense}$, This calculation s more accurate in firms using straight line depreciation method. The answer is highly dependent on the types of assets used.

Total useful life of asset in years $= \dfrac{Historical\ cost}{annual\ depreciation\ expense}$, we know that historical cost is the cost of asset before deduction of any depreciation.

Remaining useful life (in years) $= \dfrac{Ending\ net\ balance\ of\ PP\&E}{Annual\ depriciation}$, we know ending net PP&E = Gross PP&E – Accumulated depreciation

The remaining useful life can also be calculated as, average depreciable life - average age

Annual capital expenditures to depreciation expense ratio: another common measure used by analysts to determine whether the firm is replacing its PP&E at the same rate as its assets are being depreciated.

LOS 28n: Compare the financial reporting of investment property with that of property plant and equipment.

In this section we are required to differentiate between the reporting of investment property and the property plant and equipment.

Remember this only applies to companies reporting under IFRS. U. S. GAAP does not distinguish between investment property and other long-lived assets.

Under IFRS Investment property must be valued using either the cost model or the fair value model. But whatever we have decided, we have to stick with it for all investment properties. We can't decide on asset by asset which model to work with.

The cost model we've seen before with other long-lived assets. And for investment properties there is no difference in the accounting treatment.

The fair value model is different from the revaluation model we looked at earlier in this section.

The revaluation model required us to post certain types of asset value increases to shareholders equity in an account called the revaluation surplus. The fair value model requires that we post any gains directly to the income statement.

One final thing to consider here is the accounting treatment of transferring an asset between classifications.

What do we do if we want to reclassify an asset from investment property to PP&E or vice versa? If we currently hold the asset as part of PP&E using the fair value method, we treat the transfer like a revaluation. So, the reported value of PP&E is the fair value at the day of revaluation less any subsequent accumulated depreciation. For assets transferred from investment property to PP&E, we take the asset`s fair value at time of transfer and use that as the asset`s cost basis for future reporting as part of PP&E.

LOS 28 o: Explain and evaluate how leasing rather than purchasing assets affects financial statements and ratios.

LOS 28p: Explain and evaluate how finance leases and operating leases affect financial statement and ratios from perspective of both the lessor and the lessee.

Lease: Lease is a contractual agreement between lessor (the owner of asset) and lessee (the user of asset). In this contract lessor allows the lessee to use the asset for a specified time with periodic payments in return.

Leases are of two broad types, the finance lease (in US GAAP Finance lease is known as capital lease) and operating lease.

Finance lease: In finance lease the lessee purchase an asset by debt (periodic payments). When both parties agreed on lease contract the lessee record the amount as asset and also as a liability in balance sheet. Over the lease terms, the lessee depreciates the asset and recognizes the interest payments. This is just like purchasing of asset with borrowed money.

Operating lease: This is simply a rental agreement. No asset or liability is recorded on balance sheet. Only rental payments (expense) are recorded in income statement.

Note: The details of operating lease (future obligations) must be disclosed in financial statement footnotes.

Accounting standard bodies have decided that in 2019 the lessee`s balance sheet must show operating lease too.

Lease to be reported by lessee:

Operating lease: No entry is made at the inception of the lease (but as discussed above the future obligations must be disclosed under footnotes). Only rental income equal to lease payment is recorded in income statement as expense. In cash flow statement lease payment is recorded as cash outflow under operating activities.

Finance lease: A lower of present value of future minimum lease payments (cash outflows) or the fair value is recorded as liability and asset in balance sheet. That asset is depreciated annually. As the time goes the depreciation and interest payments are recorded as expense in income statement. Interest on lease can be calculated as,

Lease payments as beginning of period x interest rate.

In terms of cash flow statement, the total lease payment is separated as principal and interest payment. When using IFRS the principal amount goes into investing activities while interest payment can go in either financing or operating activities. Under US GAAP interest amount goes into operating activities while principal amount goes into financing activities (as outflows).

Impact of financing vs operating lease on lessee`s financial statements

	Finance lease	Operating lease
Assets	Higher	Lower
Total liabilities	Higher	Lower
Net income (at inception of lease)	Lower	Higher
Net income (in subsequent years)	Higher	Lower
EBIT	Higher	Lower
Over all net income (in	Same	Same

all periods)		
Operating cash flow	Higher	Lower
Cash flow from financing	Lower	Higher
Total cash flow	Same	Same

Impact of financing vs operating lease on lessee`s ratios

	Finance lease	Operating lease
Current ratio (CA/CL)	Lower	Higher
Working capital (CA – CL)	Lower	Higher
Asset turnover (Revenue / TA)	Lower	Higher
Return on assets (in early periods) (NI / TA)	Lower	Higher
Return on equity (in early periods) (NI / SE)	Lower	Higher
Debt / Assets	Higher	Lower
Debt / Equity	Higher	Lower

In finance lease all ratios are worse. In financial statements we see some benefits like EBIT is higher (because interest is not subtracted in

EBIT calculation), CFO is higher (because principal repayments goes into CFF) and higher net income in subsequent years in finance lease.

Reporting by the Lessor

From the perspective of lessor, a lease is also classified into one of two categories, 1. Finance lease 2. Operating lease.

Finance lease: when the lease is treated as finance lease the lessor remove the asset from the balance sheet. If the lessor is manufacturer of that asset then the will recognize present value of lease payments as sale price and cost of the asset as carrying value. So, the difference between sale price and cost of asset is gross profit (as normal sale of asset).

If the lessor is not manufacturer or dealer but only providing lease then the gross profit at inception of lease is zero. It means the sale price is recognized as present value of lease payments. As at the inception of lease the asset is removed from balance sheet and an equal amount of lease receivable (equal to the present value of lease payments) is created. As the lease goes on the principal amount of lease received reduces the lease receivable (as the lessor is selling the asset at fair market value and loaned the amount to lessee). The other part of lease received (other than principal) is interest and it is recognized as interest income. In cash flow statement interest received goes into CFO and the principal (lease) reduction goes into CFI as inflow.

Operating lease: In operating lease the lessor treats it as rental income. The lessor keeps the asset in balance sheet and depreciates it.

Income Tax   Study session 8

LOS 29.a: Describe the differences between accounting profit and taxable income and define key terms, including deferred tax assets, deferred tax liabilities, valuation allowance, taxes payable, and income tax expense.

Most of the times income tax rules are different than financial statement rules. So, the income tax payable (in the perspective of income tax authorities) is may be different than recognized in income statement.

Some most common terminologies of income tax

Taxable income: *It is* the base income on which *income* tax authorities imposes tax. It is the income on which the tax is deductible by law.

Taxes payable: it is the liability arises from taxable income. It is the current tax expense calculated from taxable income according the tax laws.

Income tax paid: It is the actual outflow from income as tax expense.

Tax loss carried forward: it is the current or past losses that can be used to reduce taxable income (and current tax payable) in future. It causes deferred tax liability.
<u>Tax base:</u> amount of an asset or liability used for tax calculation and reporting purpose.

Financial reporting terminologies related to income tax:

Accounting profit: It is also called income before tax or earnings before tax. This is pre-tax income calculated according to the financial accounting standards.

Income tax expense: Income tax expense = taxes payable + changes in deferred tax liabilities – changes in deferred tax asset. It is the income tax recognized in financial statements (income tax and any changes in deferred tax liabilities and assets)

Deferred tax liabilities: This is a balance sheet item. It shows any excess of income tax expense over income taxes payable. it is expected to be paid in future. A very good example for this is when a company chose to use accelerated depreciation for tax purpose but uses straight line method for financial reporting. Using accelerated depreciation method, the depreciation expense will be higher in first periods and the tax payable would be less. Off course the tax payable would be higher in later periods. For this company choose to recognize higher tax payable in first periods so the affect will be offset in coming years.

Deferred tax assets: This is a balance sheet item. It shows any excess of income tax payable over income taxes expense. it is expected to be recovered in future. When this happens, we carry forward tax loss.

Valuation allowance: When deferred tax asset is not likely to be realized we reduce the asset. That reduction is called valuation allowance.

Carrying value: Net balance sheet value of an asset or liability.

Permanent difference: A difference between taxable income (tax return) and pretax income unlikely to reverse in the future.

Temporary difference: This is a difference between the tax base of an asset/liability and the carrying value of an asset/liability that will result in either higher or lower tax amount of tax in current period. This difference would offset in future that's why it is called temporary difference. The examples of this will come after a little bit in this section.

LOS 29.b: Explain how deferred tax liabilities and assets are created and the factors that determine how a company's deferred tax liabilities and assets should be treated for the purposes of financial analysis.

Normally the treatment of accounting items is different for tax reporting and financial reporting. This difference is due to following reasons
- The timing of revenue recognition is different for financial reporting than tax purposes.
- Some gains and or losses have difference in recognition for both.
- Some revenues are to be recognized in financial statements but cannot be recognized for tax returns, and vice versa.
- Some assets ad or liabilities have different carrying value for tax and financial reporting purposes.
- Some financial statement adjustments may not be recognized or adjusted in tax base of those items.
- Some tax losses from past can reduce future tax return.

Deferred tax liability: When income tax expense is greater than taxes payable due to temporary differences the deferred tax liability is created (it has to be paid in future). It can be caused by following reasons:
- Revenues and or gains are recognized in the income statement but not yet included on the tax return due to temporary differences.
- Expenses and or losses are used to tax deduction but not are recognized in the income statement.

A most common cause of deferred tax liability is when an accelerated depreciation method is used on the tax purposes but straight-line depreciation method is used in the income statement.

Deferred Tax Assets: When taxes payable are greater than income tax expense (in income statement) due to temporary differences a deferred tax asset is created. Following reason can cause deferred tax asset creation:
- Revenues and or gains are not yet recognized in the income Statement but used for tax purposes.
- Expenses and or losses are recognized in the income statement but not yet used for tax deduction.
- Carried forward losses reduce future taxable income.
Tax loss carry forwards are used to reduce future taxable income.

Treatment for Analytical Purposes
If deferred tax liabilities are to reverse in the future, they should be treated as liabilities (for analysis). if not, they must be classified as equity
The analyst has to decide when and why we should treat them as liability or equity on case by case basis.

LOS 29.c: Calculate the tax base of a company's assets and liabilities.

Tax Base of Assets: This is the value attributed to an asset for tax purposes. If that asset is sold that amount (tax base) is tax deductible.

Carrying value of asset: It is the net value an asset reported in financial statements. Carrying value of asset = Cost of asset − accumulated depreciation or amortization − any impairment if occurred.

Calculation of tax base of assets

Accounts receivable: Let`s say a firm is having receivables of $ 10000. As the collection is uncertain the firm recognize the bad debts reserve of $1ooo. But tax authorities do not recognize bad debt reserve unless it they actually occurred (they seem worthless). At the end of one year the tax base is $10000 but the carrying value is $9000, (10000-1000). So, the deferred tax asset is created. When the bad debts are not collectable in second period they would be tax deductible.

Depreciable equipment: Let`s say the cost of equipment is $5000. The firm recognizes depreciation expense of $500 in income statement for 10 years. For tax purposes, the asset is depreciated at $1000 per year for five years. After the end of first period (year) the tax base of asset is $4000 (5000-1000) while the carrying value of asset is 5000-500 =$4500. A deferred tax liability of ($1,000 × tax rate) is created to account for the timing difference from different depreciation for tax and for financial reporting.

Tax Base of Liabilities: Tax base of a liability = carrying value of the liability - any amounts that will be deductible on the tax return in the future.

Calculation of tax base of liabilities

Advance payment by customer: Let`s say, a customer bought goods for $1000 from our firm and paid in advance. The goods have to be shipped next year. For taxation purposes revenues received in advance are taxable. But for our firm $1000 is a liability. The carrying value of this liability is $1000. Next year when we ship the goods, this liability would be removed.

We know that, Tax base of a liability = carrying value of the liability - any amounts that will be deductible on the tax return in the future.

The advance is already taxed and will not be taxable in future, the tax base of this liability is zero now ($1000 -$1000). As we have paid tax on $1000 but have not yet reported on income statement and it will cause a future deduction in tax, a deferred tax asset is created.

Delay in expense recognition: Some expenses like Warranties are recognized in income statement but for tax return they are only tax deductible when actually expensed. If for example a firm estimate that $1000 of warranty expense are required for next year for the goods sold this year.

The tax authorities do not allow to deduct warranties unless it is actually performed. The carrying value of warranty liability is $1000. The tax base = carrying value – any amount deductible I future. So, the 1000 – 1000 = 0 is the tax base. In this case the expense is recognized in delay. So, a deferred tax asset is created.

Note payable. Notes payables are treated for tax and income statements alike. So, no deferred asset or liability is created in this case. As there is not delayed or early recognition of expense.

LOS 29.d: Calculate income tax expense, income taxes payable, deferred tax assets, and deferred tax liabilities, and calculate and interpret the adjustment to the financial statements related to a change in the income tax rate.

Deferred tax liability: Let`s say an asset`s original cost is $100000. The depreciation method for tax purpose is accelerated depreciation method. The depreciation expense using this method is 40000, 30000, 20000 and 10000 for year 1, 2, 3 and 4 respectively. While the firm is using straight line method for financial reporting, following table shows income statement items for financial purpose (using straight line method at 25% depreciation rate). The tax rate is 20%.

	YEAR 1	year 2	year 3	year 4	year 1-4
EBITDA	700000	700000	700000	700000	2800000
Depreciation (SL)	25000	25000	25000	25000	100000
Pre tax income	675000	675000	675000	675000	2700000
Tax rate	20%	20%	20%	20%	20%
Tax payable	135000	135000	135000	135000	540000
Income after tax	540000	540000	540000	540000	2160000

The following table shows income statement items by using accelerated method

EBITDA	700000	700000	700000	700000	2800000
Depreciation (AR)	40000	30000	20000	10000	100000
Pre tax income	660000	670000	680000	690000	2700000
Tax rate	20%	20%	20%	20%	20%
Tax payable	132000	134000	136000	138000	540000
Income after tax	528000	536000	544000	552000	216000ᴕ

In year 1, firm recognized income tax expense of 135000 but they actually paid 132000 as tax return. So, a difference of 3000 is recorded in balance sheet as deferred tax liability because income tax expense in higher that actually paid tax. We can calculate deferred tax liability from income tax expense and tax return (tax payable). At the end of first year the carrying value of asset is 75000 (i.e. 100000-25000) but tax base of asset is 60000 (i.e. 100000- 40000). The difference between asset`s carrying value and tax base is 15000. We multiply the difference by tax rate (15000 x .20) we get 3000 DTL.

In year two the tax expense is 135000 but tax return is 134000. 1000 difference would go into balance sheet as dtl (added in previous balance). So, the tax expense for year 2 is tax return plus any change in dtl. Which is 134000 + 1000 = 135000. In year 3 tax expense is still 135000 but tax return is 136000. So, the tax expense for year 3 would be tax return + change in dtl. We are paying 1000 more than our income tax expense so tax expense would be 136000 + (-1000) = 135000. In year 4 all the dtl would reverse and we end up by paying same total income tax expense as if would use same depreciation methods for both (financial reporting and tax return).

Deferred tax Asset: Now if we inverse the above-mentioned examples we can understand deferred tax asset. Using the same example in other way let`s just say the accelerated depreciation methods is used for financial reporting while for tax return we use straight line depreciation method. All the other data remains same. At the end of first year tax payable is 132000 while tax return is 135000. Since this difference is temporary a deferred tax asset is created. In second year the tax payable is 134000 but tax return is 135000 again. This again adds up the deferred tax asset. In third year the tax expense is 136000 and tax return is 135000 which reverse the deferred tax asset. At the end of year 4 all the DTA is reverse and we end up paying same total tax return.

LOS 29.e: Evaluate the effect of tax rate changes on a company's financial statements and ratios.

A change in tax rate changes the DTA and DTL. And increase (decrease) in tax rate will increase (decrease) DTA and DTL. Changes in DTA and DTL will affect the income tax expense for current period.
As we know that;
income tax expense = taxes payable + ΔDTL −ΔDTA

We take the same example used in LOS 30d. What would happen if tax rate changes from 20% to 30%? We know that the tax base of asset in year 1 is 100000-40000 = 60000 while carrying value is 75000. The difference is 15000. Previously the DTL was 15000x 20% = 3000. With a change in tax rate new DTL would be 15000 x 30% = 4500.

AS DTA and DTL are balance sheet items so any ratio comes up with assets or liabilities would be affected by changes in DTA and DTL.

LOS 29.f: Distinguish between temporary and permanent differences in pre-tax accounting income and taxable income.

Temporary difference: A temporary difference between pre-tax accounting income and taxable income is a difference that will reverse in future. Temporary difference creates deferred tax asset or deferred tax liability. It happens due to the timing difference of revenues and or expense recognition in tax rules and accounting rules. Tax rule may recognize an expense later than accounting rules or tax rules may recognize income earlier than accounting rules.
Temporary difference can be of two types

Taxable temporary difference: This results in future taxable income. In this case we create deferred tax liability.

Deductible temporary difference: This results in future tax deductions. In this case we had created deferred tax asset.

Permanent difference: A permanent difference is a difference between taxable income and pretax accounting income that will not reverse in future. So, it does not create deferred tax asset or deferred tax liability. Permanent difference may be a result of an un-taxable revenues or not deductible expense. It can also be a result of tax credit. Permanent difference can create a difference between firm`s effective tax rate and statutory tax rate.

Statutory tax rate: It is the tax rate of jurisdiction where firm operates. Effective tax rate: It is derived from the formula,

$$Effective\ tax\ rate = \frac{income\ tax\ expense}{pre\ tax\ accountin\ income}$$

LOS 29g: Describe the valuation allowance for deferred tax assets, when it is required and what effect it has on financial statements.

We know that deferred tax assets are created from temporary differences that would reverse in future.

According to US GAAP if there are more than 50 % chances that the deferred tax asset will not reverse fully or partially in future due to insufficient taxable income, a valuation account is created (valuation allowance is only created for DTA).

Valuation account is a contra account that reduces the net balance sheet DTA, reduces net income (by increasing income tax expense). If in subsequent periods the circumstances changed the valuation allowance can be decreased to increase DTA (which will increase net income).

It is up to management to use valuation allowance. If they are earning sufficient income valuation allowance is not required. But if they have a history of inadequate earnings (so, they could not carry forward income tax losses) they should maintain valuation allowance.

We know increasing valuation allowance reduces net income and vice versa, management can manipulate earnings by using this allowance. Whenever a company reports huge DTA (and or valuation allowance) analyst must review firm`s performance to judge whether they are going to realize DFA or not. Analyst must also analyze that a huge change in valuation allowance must be economically justifies.

Under IFRS no valuation allowance is maintained. We only reduce or increase DTA directly.

LOS 29h: Explain recognition and measurement of current and deferred tax items.

- Current tax payables or recoverable depends upon current tax rate.
- The Deferred tax assets and liabilities are created due to temporary differences. Their measurement depends upon the future tax rate when the difference is going to reverse or deferred tax items are going to settle.
- All the deferred tax items (assets and liabilities) must be re assessed and measured according to their probable future economic benefits. For example, if the future taxable income is expected to be lower than the DTA and liability must be adjusted accordingly.
- If deferred tax liability is expected not to reverse in future it must be treated as equity by analyst. (DTL is not going to reverse due to any reason).
- If there is uncertainty in tax payments (timing of payment and amount of tax) analyst should exclude DTL from analysis (do not consider it as liability or equity).

LOS 29i: Analyze disclosures relating to deferred tax items and the effective tax rate reconciliation and explain how information included in these disclosures affects a company's financial statements and financial ratios.

Disclosure: Following information is required to be disclosed relating to deferred tax items,
- Deferred tax assets and liabilities, valuation allowance and net change in valuation allowance over time.
- Unrecognized deferred tax liability (if any) for undistributed earnings.
- Effect of current year tax on temporary difference (and on DTA, DTL).
- Components of income tax expense.
- Reconciliation of reported income tax expense and the tax expense based.
- Tax loss carry forwards.

Analysis of effective tax rate reconciliation

Sometimes reported income tax expense is different from the amount based on statutory income tax rate. We know that statutory tax rate is the tax rate that is imposed by law in that area. Following could be the reasons of those differences.

- Difference in tax rate in different jurisdictions.
- Permanent tax differences like tax exemptions, tax credits, none deductible expenses, and difference between operating income and capital gains.
- Changes in tax laws of the jurisdictions in which firm or its subsidiary operate.
- Deferred tax assets arise from reinvestment of earnings of foreign and domestic affiliates.
- Tax holidays

An analyst has to understand each of these reconciliation items, their impact on future earnings, its past changes and expected future changes in these elements.

Its also important for analyst to include only those items in her analysis which are continuous in nature. For example, different tax rates in different states (or countries) income exempted from tax, tax credits, none deductible expenses are continuous in nature. While tax holidays and capital gain taxes are periodic. The footnotes and MD &A should be reviewed to understand the nature of an item.

LOS 29j: Identify the key provisions of and differences between income tax accounting under International Financial Reporting Standards (IFRS) and US generally accepted accounting principles (GAAP).

Accounting treatment of income tax under US GAAP and IFRS is mostly similar. The differences are stated as under,

Upward Revaluation: under US GAAP upward revaluation is not allowed. Under IFRS upward is permitted and results in equity.

Valuation allowance: under US GAAP we maintain valuation allowance to offset any reduction in DTA.
Under IFRS we directly reduce DTA (no valuation allowance is needed).

Classification: Under US GAAP the classification depends on the underline asset or liability.
Under IFRS we classify DTA and DTL as none current

Non-current (long- term Liabilities) Study Session 8

Focus of the exam: In first part of this section, candidates are required to understand bond issue at par, at discount, at premium and their effect on financial statements. We should be able to calculate book value of bond and interest expense at any point of time by using effective interest. We must also be able to calculate gains and losses on bond by retiring it before maturity. In second part we are required to understand effect of lease classifications on cash flow statement, balance sheet and income statement. In third part we need to understand pension plans. In last we must be able to calculate firm`s solvency ratios.

Let`s start with bond

Bond: Bond is a debt instrument. It is a contractual promise between two parties. One is issuer of bond (borrower). Other party is lender (bond holder). The bond holder obligates the issuer to make payments (interest and principle) to bond holder over terms of the bond (until maturity). Usually this contract has two types of payments   1.periodic interest payment   2. Principle amount payment at maturity.

Some terminologies related to bond

Face value: It is the value of principle amount repaid to bondholder at maturity, also called par value. This value is used to calculate coupon payment.

Coupon rate: the interest rate stated on bond.

Coupon payment: the amount of interest periodic interest payments to bondholder. It is calculated as follows,

Coupon payment = face value x coupon rate.

Effective rate of interest: it is the rate of interest which equated present value of future cash flows of bond (interest + principle) to the issue price. (note issue price can be= <> face value). It is the rate of interest required by bondholders to cover default, liquidity and other risks. Coupon rate is usually fixed and stated on bond while effective rate is the rate actually being received by bondholders. If bond is issued at discount the effective rate is higher than coupon rate or if effective rate (or market rate is higher than coupon rate the bond is issued at discount, priced below par). If market rate is equal to coupon rate bond is issued at par (or prices at face value or priced at par). If market rate is lower than coupon rate it means bond is issued at premium (priced above par).

Balance sheet liability of a bond: It is the present value of bond`s remaining coupon payments and face value, discounted at the market rate of interest. As maturity approaches the bond liability = face value of the bond. The balance sheet liability is also known as the book value or carrying value of the bond.

Interest expense of bond: It is calculated as, book value of the bond liability at the beginning of the period x the market rate of interest at issuance.

LOS 30a: Determine the initial recognition, initial measurement and subsequent measurement of bonds.

NOTE: We are going to discuss it from the issuer`s perspective.
When the bond is issued at par:

When the bond is issued at par the yield at issuance is equal to the coupon rate of that bond. So, the present value of coupons and face value is equal to the par value. The issuance at par has following effects on financial statements.

Income statement: on the income statement interest expense is equal to coupon rate.

Balance sheet: The asset (cash received from issuance) and liability (bond) increased by the face value. The book value remains same on balance sheet over the bond`s term.

Cash flow: on the cash flow statement, when the bond is issued the proceeds are reported in cash flow from financing activities. Interest expense (the coupon payments) are recorded in CFO (under US GAAP) and in CFO or CFF (under IFRS) as outflow. As the bond matures the repayment of principle amount is recorded in CFF as outflow.
When the bond is issued at discount

When the bond yield is greater than coupon rate it is issued at discount. It means investors are going to pay less than face value of bond. It has following effects on financial statements,

Balance sheet measurement (effects on balance sheet): In case of discounted issuance the balance sheet asset and liability are increased by issuance proceeds of the bond. So, in the balance sheet, discounted bond is reported less than its face value. At any time, the book value of the bond is equal to the present value of future cash out flows (coupon and principle repayment) discounted at bond`s yield. We use bond yield at issuance.

The difference between coupon payment and interest expense (bond yield) is the amortization of discount. In each period amortization (increase) of discount is added into bond liability. So, the book value of bond and interest expense increases over time (until it reaches its face value).

When the bond is issued at premium

When the bond's yield <coupon payment rate, the bond is issued at premium. It means buyer of bond is paying more than face value. It also means the proceeds received from sale of bond are more than face value. Opposite to discount bond, a premium bond is reported at more than its face value. In each period the bond is amortized (reduced) until it reaches its face value at maturity.

LOS 30b: Describe the effective interest method and calculate interest expense, amortization of bond discounts/premiums, and interest payments.

There are two methods of accounting for bonds,   1. Straight line method
2. Effective interest method
Straight line method is not allowed under IFRS. It is only allowed under US GAAP. US GAAP still does not prefer straight line method. So effective interest method is a widely used method.

Straight line method: It is just like straight line depreciation method. Under this method the amortization of discount or premium is evenly distributed over the life of bond.

Effective interest method: In this method we use the market rate of interest or bond yield at issuance (remains constant for each period of bond). So,

Interest expense = book value of bond at issuance x bond's yield at issuance

The difference between bond yield and coupon rate is bond amortization. With effective interest method the amortization is different in each period.

The difference between coupon payment and interest expense (bond yield) is the amortization of discount. In each period amortization (increase) of discount is added into bond liability. So, the book value of bond and interest expense increases over time (until it reaches its face value).

When the bond's yield <coupon payment rate, the bond is issued at premium. It means buyer of bond is paying more than face value. It also means the proceeds received from sale of bond are more than face value. Opposite to discount bond, a premium bond is reported at more than its face value. In each period the bond is amortized (reduced) until it reaches its face value at maturity.

Coupon payment is cash item the amortization is non-cash item so it must be adjusted while presenting cash flow statement.

Under US GAAP interest paid is reported under CFO while under IFRS it is reported under either CFO or CFF.

Under US GAAP bond`s issuance cost is reported as asset and is amortized over bond`s life.

Under IFRS issuance cost reduces the value of carrying value of debt.

LOS 30c: Explain the derecognition of debt.

There are two ways to derecognize bond. When the bond matures or when the firm redeem bond before maturity.

The cash paid on maturity of bond is reported under CFF. Once the bond is mature no gain or loss is reported. Because all the discount or premium is fully amortized. It also means at maturity the face value is equal to carrying value.

Sometimes firm choose to redeem bond before its maturity. There are many reasons lead toward redemption. If interest rate falls the firm may choose to redeem costly bond. Other reasons may include huge earnings and or availability of other cheap financing opportunity (i.e. equity issuance). When the bond is redeemed gain or loss is recognized as;

Book value – redemption price. If book value is higher than redemption price gain is reported and vice versa.

If issuance cost is amortized it must be written off and adjust into gain or loss. If issuance cost was adjusted into bond liability, no separate entry is needed.

A gain or loss is reported into income statement as part of continuing operations. The analyst has to separate while forecasting the firm`s future.

In term of cash flow statement, the redemption price is reported under CFF. Gain or losses do not appear in cash flow statement using method. However, in indirect method gains is subtracted while loss is added to calculate CFO.

LOS 30d: Describe the role of debt covenants in protecting creditors.

Debt covenants: These are the restrictions imposed by lender to borrower to protect lenders interests (repayment of debt).

Debt covenants reduce the default risk so it also reduces borrowing cost. The debt covenants are of two types

1. Affirmative covenants   2. Negative covenants

Affirmative covenants: With these covenants the borrower promises to adhere certain rules imposed by lender such as

- Maintain certain level of assets as collateral.
- Insurance
- Timely payments of interest and principle amount etc.

Negative covenants: with negative covenants the borrower promises to avoid certain things that might affect borrower`s ability to repay, like

- Selling certain assets
- Issuing more debt instruments
- Acquisitions.

If borrower violates any covenant, the lender can demand immediate repayment of principle amount an any outstanding interest amount.

Analyst must understand these covenants while analyzing the bond. These covenants are recoded into footnotes.

It is also important to note to what extent these covenants restrict the issuing company while making equity analysis and future of the company.

LOS 30.e: Describe the financial statement presentation of and disclosures relating to debt.

Firms report their long-term debt in a single line in liabilities. The current portion of long term debt (interest payment and or the repayment of principle amount within one year) is reported in current liabilities. The details of long term debt are disclosed under footnotes and also in management`s discussion and analysis. The footnotes are very helpful in determining the timing and amount of the payments. The footnotes normally consist following information.

Nature and Maturity of liability dates, Coated and effective interest/ market rates, Call and conversion options, Debt covenants Assets pledged as security, the amount of debt maturing in each of the next five years.

The management`s discussion and analysis cover the quantitative and qualitative aspects of debt like obligations due and future costs of capital respectively.

LOS 30f: Explain motivations for leasing assets instead of purchasing them.

A leasing of assets is a contractual agreement between lessor (owner of asset) and lessee (user of asset) to use the asset for some specific time period in return of periodic payments.

Leases are of two broad types, the finance lease (in US GAAP Finance lease is known as capital lease) and operating lease.

Finance lease: In finance lease the lessee purchase an asset by debt (periodic payments). When both parties agreed on lease contract the lessee record the amount as asset and also as a liability in balance sheet. Over the lease terms, the lessee depreciates the asset and recognizes the interest payments. This is just like purchasing of asset with borrowed money.

Operating lease: This is simply a rental agreement. No asset or liability is recorded on balance sheet. Only rental payments (expense) are recorded in income statement.

Benefits of leasing:

- Normally in lease agreement there is no initial payments so the leasing is less costly than purchasing of asset.
- When the lease agreement ends the asset can be returned to the lender so the risk of obsolesce is reduced.
- Normally a lease agreement is more flexible than other financing modes. It can be negotiated better. So, there can be less restrictions.
- Operating lease is off balance sheet item so the leverage ratios are better.
- In US a lease can be reported as synthetic lease where lease asset is treated as owned asset (only for tax purpose). So, a tax reduction can be observed as depreciation and interest expenses are tax deductible.

LOS 30g: Distinguish between a finance lease and an operating lease from the perspectives of the lessor and the lessee.

Lessee`s perspective:

Under IFRS the lease can be classified as either operating or finance lease. The choice of classification depends upon the economic substance of the transaction. For a lease to be considered as Finance lease (under IFRS) any of the following criteria must met

- At the end pf lease title of the asset is to be transferred to lessee,
- The lessee can purchase the asset in future at significantly lower price than its fair value.

- The asset is specialized made for lessee (only the lessee can use the asset without any significant modification)
- The lease agreement covers major portion of the useful life of asset.
- The present value of payments of leased asset is significantly equal to the fair value of that asset.

US GAAP also describe some rules to classify a lease as a finance (in US GAAP Finance lease is called capital) lease. The US GAAP rules are same as IFRS but considered more specific than IFRS. For US GAAP any of the following criteria must met for finance lease;

- At the end of lease, title of the asset is to be transferred to lessee,
- The lessee can purchase the asset in future at significantly lower price than its fair value.
- A *bargain purchase option* permits the lessee to purchase the asset in future at significantly lower price than its market fair value.
- The lease agreement covers 70% or more useful life of asset.
- The present value of payments of leased asset is 90% or more to the fair value of that asset.

If none of the above criteria is met the lease is considered as operating lease. A lessee prefers operating lease in general as no asset or liability is reported in it. With finance lease lessee reports asset and liability.

Lessor`s perspective

Under IFRS the criteria for operating or finance lease is same for lessor. However, US GAAP is a little bit different here. Under U.S. GAAP, if any of the criteria of finance lease is met plus the collection of lease payments are reasonably certain then it is finance lease otherwise is treated as operating lease.

We know that with operating lease, the lessor reports rental income and depreciate the leased asset. With capital lease, the lessor removes the asset (from balance sheet) and creates a lease investment account as lease receivable.

LOS 30.h: Determine the initial recognition, initial measurement, and subsequent measurement of finance leases.

Lease to be reported by lessee:

How we treat or allowed to treat the lease (either operating or finance) has different effects on financial statements. First, we see the

Operating lease: No entry is made at the inception of the lease (but as discussed above the future obligations must be disclosed under footnotes). Only rental income (during the terms of lease) equal to lease payment is recorded in income statement as expense. In cash flow statement lease payment is recorded as cash outflow under operating activities.

Finance lease: A lower of present value of future minimum lease payments (cash outflows) or the fair value is recorded as liability and asset in balance sheet. That asset is depreciated annually. As the time goes the depreciation and interest payments are recorded as expense in income statement. Interest on lease can be calculated as,

Lease payments as beginning of period x interest rate.

In terms of cash flow statement, the total lease payment is separated as principal and interest payment. When using IFRS the principal amount goes into investing activities while interest payment can go in either financing or operating activities. Under US GAAP interest amount goes into operating activities while principal amount goes into financing activities (as outflows).

Impact of financing vs operating lease on lessee`s financial statements

	Finance lease	Operating lease
Assets	Higher	Lower
Total liabilities	Higher	Lower
Net income (at inception of lease)	Lower	Higher
Net income (in subsequent years)	Higher	Lower
EBIT	Higher	Lower
Over all net income (in all periods)	Same	Same
Operating cash flow	Higher	Lower
Cash flow from financing	Lower	Higher
Total cash flow	Same	Same

Impact of financing vs operating lease on lessee`s ratios

	Finance lease	Operating lease
Current ratio (CA/CL)	Lower	Higher
Working capital (CA – CL)	Lower	Higher
Asset turnover (Revenue / TA)	Lower	Higher
Return on assets (in early periods) (NI / TA)	Lower	Higher
Return on equity (in early periods) (NI / SE)	Lower	Higher
Debt / Assets	Higher	Lower
Debt / Equity	Higher	Lower

Reporting by the Lessor
From the perspective of lessor, a lease is also classified into one of two categories, 1. Finance lease 2. Operating lease.

Finance lease: when the lease is treated as finance lease the lessor remove the asset from the balance sheet. If the lessor is manufacturer of that asset then the will recognize present value of lease payments as sale price and cost of the asset as carrying value. So, the difference between sale price and cost of asset is gross profit (as normal sale of asset).

If the lessor is not manufacturer or dealer but only providing lease then the gross profit at inception of lease is zero. It means the sale price is recognized as present value of lease payments. As at the inception of lease the asset is removed from balance sheet and an equal amount of lease receivable (equal to the present value of lease payments) is created. As the lease goes on the principal amount of lease received reduces the lease receivable (as the lessor is selling the asset at fair market value and loaned the amount to lessee). The other part of lease received (other than principal) is interest and it is recognized as interest income.

In cash flow statement interest received goes into CFO and the principal (lease) reduction goes into CFI as inflow.

Operating lease: In operating lease the lessor treats it as rental income. The lessor keeps the asset in balance sheet and depreciates it.

From Lessor`s perspective, Under US GAAP a capital lease is either treated as sale type lease or direct financing lease.
Sale type lease: If Pv of lease payments > asset`s carrying value, the lease is treated as sale type lease.
Direct financing lease: If Pv of lease payments = asset`s carrying value, the lease is treated as direct financing lease.

Note: IFRS does not differentiate this treatment but allows to treat a lease like sale type if it is directly from manufacturer or dealer of asset.

Sales-Type Lease: A lease is treated as sale type if the carrying value (balance sheet value) is less than fair value of the asset and the lessor is manufacturer or dealer of leased asset. It is like as if the lessor sold the asset to lessee at present value of leased payments and financed the same item (as loan) to lessee for same amount.

At the inception of lease, the lessor reports the leased asset as sale (Sale = present value of lease payments) and cost equal to the caring value of the asset. The difference in sale and cost value is recognized as gross profit. The leased asset is removed from balance sheet and another asset of lease receivable is created (of course equal to the present value of lease payments). When the lease installment is received the asset is reduced by principle amount and the extra amount from principle amount is recognized as interest income. Interest income = lease receivables at beginning of period x lease interest rate.

In cash flow statement we record interest received under CFO while principle under CFI.

Direct Financing Lease: When the carrying value is equal to the present value of leased payments it is treated as direct financing so, no gross profit is recognized under this treatment (because PV of lease payments = carrying value of asset). It this case the lessor is normally not a manufacturer or dealer but a third-party purchaser of asset.

When lease happens, the asset is removed from lessor`s balance sheet and another asset named lease receivables is created with same amount (carrying value). Whenever lease payment is received the lease receivable is reduced by principle amount and interest received is recorded into income statement. Interest amount is equal to lease receivable at beginning of period x leased interest rate. In cash flow statement the interest income is recorded in CFO and principle in CFI.

Operating lease: In operating lease the lessor treats it as rental income. The lessor keeps the asset in balance sheet and depreciates it.

LOS 30i: Compare the disclosures relating to finance and operating leases.

The lessor and lessee are required to disclose useful information about lease agreement in financial statements and or in footnotes. The information must include followings,

---

- Description of lease agreement in general.
- In each of next five years what is the nature,
- Amount and timings of lease payments/ receipts.
- The amount to be paid after five years can be disclosed as total.
- Amount received and unearned revenues from lease.
- Restrictions imposed in lease agreement.

LOS 30j: Compare the presentation and disclosure of defined contribution and defined benefit pension plans.

Pension: It is the amount of funds collected from employees during their services. These funds are used to support the person after retirement.

The two broad categories of pension plan are defined contribution plan and defined pension plan.

Defined contribution plan: It is a retirement plan in which employer contributes a certain amount of money in each period (i.e. monthly) into employee`s retirement account. The contribution may depend on employee`s contribution, employee`s experience, duration of employee`s services etc. The employee can also contribute same or different amount. The firm provides no promises about the future value of the plan. The money is invested and it can earn positive or negative earnings. The investment decisions are left to empl0yee. The employee bears all the risks involved linked to investment.

Financial reporting requirement: Financial reporting requirements for defined contribution plan are straight forward. Amount contributed by employer is his pension expense and there is no future liability to report on balance sheet.

Defined benefit plan: It is a retirement plan in which the employer assumes risk of future value of the plan. The employer promises to pay certain periodic payments to employee in future (after retirement). In this plan the employer contributes certain amount (the employee may or may not contribute) into fund and generally sends the amount to an institution which is specialized for investment. The employer makes sure a certain future value of the fund. The retirement benefits usually depend on employee`s years of service, or the compensations at retirement. For example, an employee who is to be entitled 3% of her salary (0f $200000) and served for 30 years may get

200000 x 30 x 2% = $120000

Financial reporting requirement: Financial reporting is complicated here. The employer needs to estimate value of future obligation of defined benefit plan. The variables used to forecast are mortality rate, future compensation amount (salary), retirement age and discount rate.

If the fair value of plan asset is greater than future obligation then plan Is called <u>overfunded</u> plan and <u>an asset named net pension</u> is to be recorded into balance sheet of employer. On the other hand, if fair value is less than pension obligation the plan is called <u>underfunded</u> and the employer has to record <u>net pension liability</u> in balance sheet.

Reporting under IFRS

1. Service cost/past service cost + Interest income/ expense go into Income statement (under pension expense)

3. Re-measurement +Actuarial gains/losses + Actual return + Expected return go into   Balance sheet (under shareholder`s equity)

Reporting under US GAAP

1. Service cost/past service cost + Interest income/ expense go into Income statement (under pension expense).
2. Expected return on assets +Actuarial gains/losses go into   Balance sheet (under shareholder`s equity) (the amortization of expected return on assets +Actuarial gains/losses goes back into income statement as expense.

First, we need to define these terms;
Service cost: It is the present value of the retirement benefits which employee is entitled to take in current year.
Past service costs: It is the changes in the value of defined benefit plan in previous periods. Interest expense or interest income is equal to the value of asset in the beginning of the year x interest rate.
The interest rate depends on the management`s judgment but it should reflect the yield rate of A rated bond.
Actuarial gains and losses are the difference between the actual pension payments and the expected amount. Actuarial gain = amount paid < expected. Actuarial loss = amount paid > expected.

Under IFRS

Any change in net liability or asset is calculated and annually calculated and reported in financial statements. These changes are recorded in other comprehensive income, in net income or in balance sheet. Under IFRS service cost, interest expense, expected return on plan assets goes into income statement, and then goes to balance sheet ultimately. On the other hand, past services cost, actuarial gains or losses goes into balance sheet.

Under US GAAP
Under US GAAP there are five parts of net pension asset or liability. Service costs, net interest expense, and the expected return are the net pension expense goes into income statement.

Past service costs and actuarial gains or losses goes into other comprehensive income. These two are amortized into current pension expense annually. It means the firm can report their pension expense and net pension obligation over the term of the life of plan.

For a manufacturing firm the IFRS and US GAAP pension expense is allocated to cost of goods sold and inventory (for direct labor) and to administrative expenses and salaries (for administrative services). Therefore, pension expense does not show in income statement. Footnotes must be examined carefully to understand the pension expense.

LOS 30k: Calculate and interpret leverage and coverage ratios.

Leverage ratios: In leverage ratios we use balance sheet items to calculate debt amount in firm`s capital structure.

Some terms are needed to be understood first
Total debt: In leverage ratios total debt means all interest-bearing liabilities (i.e. loan from bank). All other liabilities which do not bear interest are not included like payables, deferred tax etc.
Total assets: These are all current and long-term assets.
Total capital= total debt + equity
Average total assets= {total assets in previous year + total assets current year} /2
Average equity= {equity in previous year + equity in current year} /2

Leverage ratios
Debt to assets ratio= total debt / total assets.
It measures the percentage of total assets which are being financed with debt. A less than 50 percentage is good.
Debt to capital ratio= total debt / total capital

It is a measure of the percentage of total capital financed by debt.

Debt to equity ratio= total debt / total equity.

It measures the amount of debt financing relative to the firm's equity financing. If this ratio is 1 it means the firm has equal amounts of debt and equity. Means 50 % capital came from equity and other 50% from debt.

Financial leverage ratio= average total assets / average total equity.

It measures how much assets a company has relative to its equity. Higher the ratio higher the leverage and riskier the firm is.

All the leverage ratios must be lower or equal to the industry norms. A higher of any of these ratios means higher leverage and more risk.

Coverage ratios

With coverage ratios we use income statement element to measure adequacy of earnings to cover fixed charges like interest payments.

Interest coverage ratio= EBIT / interest payments.

Higher of this ratio is desirable. If this ratio is lower, then firm is experiencing difficulty in interest payment.

Fixed charge coverage ratio = (EBIT + lease payments) / (interest payments + lease payments).

This is like interest coverage ratio but also consider lease payments too. It should also be higher.

Financial reporting quality Study session 9

LOS 31a: Distinguish between financial reporting quality and quality of reported results (including quality of earnings, cash flow, and balance sheet items).

Financial reporting quality: Financial reporting quality is the usefulness of a financial document / set of financial documents for those who need to make decisions about the firm. Generally, users of financial documents are investors, creditors, potential business partners etc.

Financial documents are useful if they fulfill following conditions
- Relevance
- Timeliness
- Faithful representation.

Relevance means the information generated by financial documents must impact the decision making of users of these documents. Relevance also means the information must be material.

Timeliness means the information must be provided in time when the users need to make decisions about the company.

Faithful representation means completeness, neutrality, and the absence of errors.

Quality of reported results: It means sustainability and level of earnings. How sustainable the business is to produce this level of earnings. Higher earnings due to the events which are not likely to occur (like changes in exchange rate) in future does not means a sustainable level of earnings. On the other hand, attaining efficiency and reduction in cost may lead to sustainability. A higher level of earnings means that earnings are high enough to fulfill operational needs as well as a decent return to investor.

A higher quality of financial reporting may not guarantee a higher quality of reported results. Higher quality means the financial documents are GAAP compliance but may not be sustainable.

LOS31b: Describe a spectrum for assessing financial reporting quality.

We can gauge the quality of financial reporting and quality of reported results from worst to the best.

Lowest quality financial reports: The lowest quality reports may contain fictitious entries. These are the entries which did not occur in reality but have been added intentionally to mislead users of reports. These reports are also non-GAAP compliant.

Going up from worst reporting comes the **noncompliance reporting:** These reports may be partially fictitious information but does not obey the generally accepted accounting standards. These reports may overstate or understate some items improper calculations and estimates of assets and liabilities.

GAAP compliant reports: These reports are GAAP compliant but management is using those estimates or methods (Intentionally or unintentionally) which lead towards the creation of biased reports. Biasness reduces the usability of reports and user can conclude inaccurate future estimates. Biases can be aggressive (inflated results), conservative or smoothening (to show smooth results by reducing earnings in better situations to offset bad earnings in other periods, being conservative in years of good performance and being aggressive in years of poor performance).

Reports that are GAAP compliant, decision useful but not sustainable.
It means earnings may not be expected to continue into the future and are from non-recurring activities.

GAAP compliant, decision useful and sustainable reports: It means that the reports comply with the accounting standards of the company's jurisdiction, the reports are relevant verifiable understandable and delivered in a timely manner, and earnings reported are from activities which were expected to continue into the future.

LOS 31c: Distinguish between conservative and aggressive accounting.

The unbiased and neutral financial documents are more valuable in the views of an analyst (and for other users). It means management neither uses conservative accounting nor aggressive accounting.

Conservative accounting: In conservative accounting the management tend to decrease the firm`s current earnings and financial position so reports less income and weak financial position. Use of conservatism the tendency of future earnings increases.

Aggressive accounting: If management decides to increase current earnings and financial position it is called aggressive accounting. In this method the future earnings tend to decrease.

Both aggressive and conservative accounting is not desirable. Both of these are biased and used by management to smooth their earnings (and reduce volatility) over several years.

Following are some examples of conservative vs aggressive accounting (based on management`s choices and estimates)

Aggressive	Conservative
Capitalizing cost (so the earnings would be higher)	Expensing costs (so the earning would be lower)
More useful life of assets (less depreciation expense, higher net income)	Less useful life of assets (higher depreciation less net income)
Higher salvage value (less depreciation)	Lower estimates of salvage value (more depreciation)
Declining balance or straight-line depreciation	Double accelerating depreciation method
Higher accruals of receivables (less bad debts)	Less receivable estimates (more bad debts)
Late impairment recognition	Early recognition of impairment

LOS 31d: Describe motivations that might cause management to issue financial reports that are not high quality.

LOS 31e: Describe conditions that are conducive to issuing low quality or even fraudulent financial reports.

There are three things which led management to produce low quality or even fraudulent reports,
Opportunity
Motivation
Rationalization

1. **Opportunity:** When management is given opportunity, they might take it. It mostly happens when internal controls are weak, the board is ineffective or a lack of fear about the punishment.

2. **Motivations:** There are many motivations for management to produce low quality reports. For example, when manager is trying to maintain business competitiveness by hiding a period of poor performance.
Earnings have been the most important measure in the eyes of management in terms of setting targets. Beating prior years or analyst`s expectations is a very common goal.
Sometime the motivation is to avoid a penalty from a debt covenants perspective.

3. **Rationalization:** By rationalization we mean that a person is interested in justifying their fraudulent or bias decisions.
The management seeks opportunities to justify or defend their actions. So, they believe that their choices are either in their own self-interest or in the interests of those they intend to support.

LOS 31f: Describe mechanisms that discipline financial reporting quality and the potential limitations of those mechanisms.

There are four mechanisms that contribute to the level of quality of a company's financial reports.
- Market forces and investor expectations.
- Regulatory authorities.
- Auditors
- Private contracting.

Market forces and investor expectations: We know that a company's cost of capital depends on the business risks and investor`s expectation of the risk. When a company produces low quality reports, expectation of risk is increased and investors will demand higher rate of return in order to invest or lend in than company. So, the cost of capital increases. On the other hand by persistently producing higher quality reports the cost of capital would be reduced.

Sometimes here, a conflict of interest arises. Management wants to reduce cost of capital but they might have an incentive for which they have to produce low quality reports.

Regulatory authorities: There are several authorities around the globe to establish and enforce rules and standards to protect market participants. **For example,** in Europe the European securities and markets authority, FCA the financial conduct authority in UK and SEC, the Securities and Exchange Commission in USA.

Along these there are many regional regulators and members of the IOSCO, the international organization of securities commissions, the global standard setter for the security sector.

These authorities have number of ways to influence and implement higher quality in financial reporting. For example,

Registration requirements: This means that companies have become transparent before offering securities. These regulatory authorities are a first step check on the company.

Disclosure requirements: These are several documents and their contents which a company is required to submit. Regulatory authorities have rules for these submissions and disclosures regarding those submissions.

Auditing regulators: These regulators ask the company to obtain unqualified reports of independent auditors to ensure best accounting practices.

Enforcement power of regular: Regulatory authorities have power to fine, power to suspend for any wrong doing of the companies.

A limitation is to be discussed here. If a regulator is not strong enough he may not be able to ensure high quality reports to the users.

Auditors: This is the simplest of four mechanisms. When an independent auditor cleared the financial documents, the users get some assurance that the proper methods of estimates, disclosures and related accounting standards have been followed.

Regrettably, the work of auditor is limited. It is limited to the information provided to the auditor. If management deliberately mislead the auditor the auditor`s report might also be misleading.

Mostly auditor`s opinion is based on a sample of accounts. If the fraud is hided in depth, it might be hard for auditor to detect.

The auditors do not seek out fraudulent activity intentionally. They use designated set of processes to check if the reports are accounting standard compliant and fair.

Private contracting: Private contracting parties is another important source for financial discipline. For example, a lending party would calculate different financial measures and come up with better interpretations. Parties who do business with a particular company have an incentive to look closely in their business affairs.

A limitation here, when there is penalty from lenders, for certain events like lower earnings the borrower has some incentive to produce low quality reports.

LOS 31g: Describe presentation choices including non-GAAP measures that could be used to influence an analyst`s opinion.

Accounting choices (in calculation and presentation of financial data) made in financial reporting must be understood by analyst in order to evaluate company`s financial reports. These choices affect usefulness of reports.

Sometimes firms use some measures not defined in GAAP or not required in GAAP to look financial reports better. Normally these are excluded from financial reports. Justifications given by management for this exclusion include
- These items are of non-recurring
- They are non-cash items
- By excluding these items, they are improving comparability.

In US the firms which uses non-GAAP measures are required to disclose following
Show the most comparable GAAP measure with same prominence
Give justification why non-GAAP measure is useful
Reconcile/ ratify the difference between non-GAAP and comparable GAAP measure
Purpose of using non-GAAP measure

IFRS requires following to be disclosed for using non IFRS measures
Relevance of such measure
Reconcile the difference between non IFRS and most comparable IFRS measure

Here is an example of non-GAAP measure from which you will have quite the idea.

A company is downsizing and expensing much on it. They may exclude these expenses and show more information on operations for paint a good picture.

LOS31h: Describe accounting methods choices and estimates that could be used to manage earnings, cash flow and balance sheet items.

There are various ways by which management can change results and show better results in their financial reports. Through these methods they can affect the balance sheet, income statement and cash flows.

Some of these methods are used to gear up a below normal performance and other can reduce the results.

Choices affecting balance sheet: We must be looking in
- Revenue recognition.
- Inventory management.
- Accrual accounting
- Deferred tax assets.
- Depreciation.
- Capitalization of expenses.

Revenue recognition: It means management is recognizing revenues early or delaying them according to their need.

For example, we have a huge order to export goods at the end of a period. We need to recognize the earnings when the title and responsibilities of ordered goods have been transferred. But in order to make things look better management decides to recognize the revenues before the end of the period (and before the transfer of responsibility) they are influencing the revenues for the current period.

Inventory: How the management is recording cost of goods sold and ending inventory in the accounts.

We have three methods, **FIFO** first in first out, weighted average cost, LIFO method last in first out.

When prices are going up use of FIFO gives us out of dated cost of goods sold but a better inventory in hand (inventory value is according to current market prices). This makes the balance sheet look better.

By using weighted average method, the cost of goods sold is somewhat closer to the current fair value but the balance sheet is not as close to the current market value of inventory (as it was with the use of FIFO). Management has opportunity here to engineer the balance sheet according to their need.

LIFO is not permitted under IFRS so let's not discuss it here as we have discussed it in detail before. I think we got the idea how inventory method can be used by management in their favor.

Accrual accounting: It is a method of reporting current period activity as opposed to current period cash. It means revenues and expenses should be recognized when they occur irrespective to cash may or may not change hands.

Management can use this approach in their favor to manipulate results. When a firm sold the goods, they have receivables. They need to maintain a provision for bad debts and fair value of collectibles. These two items are subject to the judgment of management.

Deferred tax assets: After experiencing a loss, the management creates an account of deferred tax asset in their balance sheet. When they will be in profit

They will use that deferred tax asset to reduce their tax bill. This is true for a startup companies and the successful companies who hit a loss accidently. But what if a company is in decline and will be getting out of business in next four or five year they may not use their entire deferred tax asset. This is also a subjective approach and is on management's discretion.

Depreciation methods: It is an allocation of the cost of a long-lived asset to the several years.

There are three major methods.
- Straight line.
- Accelerated.
- Activity based.

And we also have to estimate salvage value.

The choice of depreciation method and estimates about salvage value depends on management. The different choice may lead towards different results.

Capitalization: It means firm has to decide whether the expense they made is going to give them benefit in one year or in multiple years.

Sometimes management delays the current expenses by capitalizing to show better earnings in current period.

Accounting choices to influence the statement of cash flow.

Statement of cash flow has three parts
- CFO, operating cash flows.
- CFI, cash flows from investment activities.
- CFF, cash flow from financing activities.

Within cash flow statement, CFO is of most importance to check earnings of the firm. With respect to accruals and depreciation, cash flows are less likely to be manipulated.

First of all, we need to check relationship between net income and operating cash flow.

If amount of cash generated in a period > net income, we have good quality earnings and financial reports.

If amount of cash generated in a period < net income, we have bad quality earnings and financial reports.

When cash inflow is far low from net earnings it means management did something to report higher earnings than actual reality.

The company management knows lower inflow from operation will look bad, they also use some methods to raise cash inflow. The most common way of doing this is managing account payables. What if management wants to show more cash in hand by delaying payment to their supplier. They will be raising account payables but cash position would be higher. They can fool us if we only see at cash position and ignore payables.

Sometimes management decides to show improved cash flow by **misclassifying items** from investing or financing activities. In this method they bring inflow items in CFO. Sometimes management constructs a complex transaction/agreement to confuse user which is also a bad sign.

LOS31i: Describe accounting warning signs and methods for detecting manipulation of information in financial reports.

In this LOS we will be looking at
- Revenues,
- Inventory,

- Capitalization,
- Relationship between net income and cash flow,
- Fourth quarter earnings
- Non-recurring entries.

Revenues: This is the item which is the number one source of manipulation. So, we have to look at this item first. First of all we need to look at the notes for management policies regarding revenue recognition, rebates etc. Any suspicious entry here would be a bad start

If a company has outperformed comparative to their peers and competitors we need to check it. Does this performance is achieved through superior management, superior product or through manipulation.
If the firm has outperformed deviated from its historical trends we need to check for a reasonable explanation.
After that we need to check ratios like receivables turnover, days sales outstanding, asset turnover and compare them to the industry norms.

Inventory: The firms who holds inventory has significant opportunities to manipulate it. We must check and compare inventory figure with industry norms and the company`s own historical trends. Anything unusual must be checked for reasonable explanation.
Inventory turnover ratios must also be checked. A declining inventory turnover might indicate threat of obsolescence. We should compare it with industry norms and the company`s historical trends and or a reasonable explanation.

Capitalization: It also means deferring of costs. First of all, check the notes regarding policies relating to capitalization. Compare these policies with industry norms. If difference appears check out asset turnover and profitability ratios for comparability.

Relationship between net income and cash flow: Cash inflows plays very critical role for a company to perform well and even to survive. When a firm is aggressively capitalizing cost (means delaying cost as expense) they are showing higher income for current period.   Same results can also be achieved by aggressive accrual accounting. If cash is not coming in despite higher earnings it must get the analyst into suspicion. We need to calculate percentage of cash inflow with respect to income (cash inflow/ income) over a number of years to see the trends. If cash inflow percentage declines it's a red flag and analyst must demand or seek further investigation.

Fourth quarter earnings: we need to look at 4th quarter earnings. are they match with previous quarter`s earnings or not? (Of course we must consider the element of seasonality).

Non-recurring or one-off items: We need to look closely for non-recurring items if they recur again and again and vice versa. For example, a huge cash inflow from non-recurring item, stated into income from operations and an expense stated into non-recurring expense but coming into accounts several times.

Financial Statement Analysis: Applications

Study Session 9

LOS 32a: Evaluate a company's past financial performance and explain how a company`s strategy is reflected in past financial performance.

In evaluation of past performance, we are interested in how things have changed with the passage of time. We not only check how the firm has performed but also interested in why (poor or better).

In performance evaluation first of all, we need to think about trend analysis in terms of profitability, efficiency, liquidity and solvency and any reason why they have changed.

Then this trend must be compared with industry (peers and competitors). If this firm is performing differently in comparison then why?

Secondly, we need to understand what are the factors for success in this industry and where does this firm stand.

Thirdly what is the model of this firm, its competitive strategy, and how management is able to grow profitability and get more efficiency.

For answers to all above mentioned questions we need to look at company`s financial statements, disclosures and proxies like investor relations department, Corporate press releases, and related information analyst can get by visiting company. We also need to look at industry information, trade surveys, publications etc.

After getting all the information we perform various analysis tools like
- Common size financial statements.
- Financial ratios
- Compare with industry specific metrics.

After performing analysis tool, we need to understand and conclude.

For example, if our firm under consideration is in business of premium products, they must be selling at high profit margin and lower cost of goods sold, higher research and development costs etc. So, all these elements must be seen in the financial statements of our firm.

LOS 32b: Forecast the company's future net income and cash flow.

Reason for future projection: Projections of a company`s cash flows are used for credit analysis. The most common users of this projections are future and current lenders and or partners to understand company`s default risk.

Data: The data would be internal (company`s financial statements), industrial outlook, and macro-economic variables etc.

Past performance is very useful in terms of a guide to forecast future for a stable and well diversified company. But a company with a volatile and new company past performance may not be a very useful item to consider.

We generally have two types of future forecasts
- Short term/ near term
- Long term/ multi period

First of all, we must forecast company`s sales. To forecast sales, we use top down approach in short term projections.

With this approach first, we forecast industry sales revenue. We use regression analysis to built relationship between industry overall sales revenue and some macro indicator like real GDP. With industry sale forecast we forecast our company`s sale revenues by considering our company`s share in the market. If the future market share of the company we are taking into consideration is going to change we need to adjust it too.

Next, we forecast expenses. (Sometimes we avoid expense forecasting and go direct for gross profit margin by historical trend, historical trend is more useful in well diversified and stable companies).

To forecast net profit, we need to consider financial leverage and tax effects. We can also forecast net profit margin (like gross profit but disadvantage is same).

In any kind of forecast beware of the following item like

Non-recurring or discontinued items must be excluded from analysis.

Restructuring charges must be ignored.

Because if we include them in model, we are expecting them to happen again which is not true.

Multi period forecast: In this forecast we use single estimate of growth rate and use it to forecast future item. For example we use 5% for sales and use it for future sales revenues.

To estimate future cash flows we need to make some assumptions of uses and sources of cash.

By building multi-period forecast we end up as follows

Income and cashflow projections

	2x10 current	2x11	2x12	2x13
Sale @4%	1200	1248	1297.9	1349.8
Less COGS @5%	600	630	661.5	694.58
Less opearting expenses@3%	200	206	212.18	218.55
Net income	400	412	424.24	436.72
Opening cash@2%	200	204	208.08	212.24
Net income	400	412	424.24	436.72
Non cash items (working capital)@75% of sales	900	936	973.44	1012.4
Ending cash	**1500**	**1552**	**1605.8**	**1661.3**

LOS32c: Describe the role of financial statement analysis in assessing the credit quality of a potential debt investment.

Credit analysis is an evaluation of credit risk. It is an analysis of an entity's ability to pay their debts.

Analyst include 3Cs 4Cs and 5Cs for credit analysis. 3Cs include character (firm`s history and reputation about debt payments), collateral (type of asset as collateral), and Capacity to repay (examination of financial statements and ratios). In 4Cs all of above plus capital (firm`s financial resources) are included. In 5Cs one more item is included in above four which is "conditions" (special conditions applicable on debt).

We know that debt must be repaid in cash analyst focus on multi-period cash flow forecast especially CFO. Because debt is to be paid from internally generated cash.

Moody's, Standard and Poor's and other credit rating companies established some formulas to rate a firm`s credibility about debt repayment. These formulas include weighted average of some ratios and business characteristics. The items include in the formula and their weight differs from industry to industry but they can be categories as under:

- Scaling and diversification.
- Tolerance for leverage
- Margin stability
- Operational efficiency

Scaling and diversification: In this category we are to look at firm`s ability to withstand in adverse economic or business conditions/event. If they have some or more control over suppliers and in market they have less credit risk.

Tolerance for leverage: In this we include interest coverage ratio and ratio of debt to total assets. A firm having better of these ratios means they have higher tolerance and lower credit risk.

Operational efficiency: Items like Return on Assets and costs are included in this section. A higher return and or lower costs better for lower credit risk.

Margins stability: It is related to variations in profit margins. Lower the variation higher the credit rating (lower credit risk).

We will discuss credit quality in detail in fixed income risk analysis.

LOS32d: Describe the use of financial statement analysis in screening for potential equity investments.

Screening means selecting a suitable portfolio from large set of stocks. Selection may involve calculations and comparing ratios.

First thing to think about is what type of investment we are looking for from growth stocks, value stocks or dividend earnings stocks.

Analysts use some ratios to select stocks. Multiple criteria must be used to select a stock for example a low price to earnings ratio is desirable but a firm cam lower price to earnings ratio if even they have declining sales or at very high leverage.

By testing the firms using historical data and ratios from that data, analyst must be aware of the biases and limitations of ratios. If these biases exist, the results cannot be trusted.

Survivorship bias: The tendency of focusing only on winners rather than losers is called survivorship bias. For example, when we are looking for a better investment fund, we include only those funds which have survived to date. May be a large number of funds have been closed due to bad performance or bitter situations. It means we are over emphasizing on a single fund and ignoring all others. This bias gives us results we cannot rely on.

Look ahead bias: This type of bias occurs when a specific data is used to test a relationship but the data was not available on that point of time. For example, while calculating price to book value for studying trading strategies the price is available at any point in time but the book value is available after 30 to 60 days of end of accounting period. One other example is restated financial statements. When the screening process was done the restated figures were not available.

Data snooping bias: This is another statistical bias and It occurs when the same data is used to test a model which was used to build that model. According to statisticians this type of bias cannot be fully eliminated.

LOS32e: Explain appropriate analyst adjustments to a company's financial statements to facilitate comparison with another company.

Most of the times analysts make some adjustments in financial statements of different companies who use different accounting choices and estimates, in order to make them comparison friendly. The difference in financial statements occurs because different companies choose different accounting methods and or different accounting standards.

In this LOS we are going to discuss some important adjustments which analyst need.

Investments in securities: Buying equity and other debt offerings of other companies is called investments in securities. It does not mean equity interests of parent company in subsidiary firm.

The management can classify investment in securities in three categories which can affect the net income differently.

These categories are
- Held for trading.
- Available for sale.
- Hold to maturity.

Held for trading:
If these securities are held for trading they must be measured at fair value and their unrealized gains and losses are reported in income statement, under US GAAP.

Available for sale:
Hold to maturity:

Under these categories the securities are measured at fair value and unrealized gains/losses are recorded in other comprehensive income in balance sheet.

Problem for arises when firms chose to classify similar securities, differently. So, analyst has to make some adjustments based on the accounting treatment for each type. Undoing the effect of one classification would make financial statements more comparable.

There is one other difference arises from choice of accounting standard (IFRS vs US GAAP). If interest rate fluctuates and there is unrealized gain/loss on held for sale securities. Under IFRS this unrealized gain/loss would be recorded in income statement. But under US GAAP that would not be the case. So, this difference would be eliminated by adding loss or subtracting gains from the income statement of IFRS firm.

Inventory: Choice of accounting treatment for inventory produces different financial results. We have FIFO, weighted average cost and LIFO (only under US GAAP) methods for inventory management.

The problem arises when one company operating under US GAAP chooses LIFO while other company under IFRS chooses weighted average or FIFO. This choice of using different inventory methods has effects on COGS and profit margins. It also affects total assets in balance sheet and equity.

Fortunately, any company reporting under LIFO method is required to disclose the value of its inventory equivalent to FIFO base. We just need to consult management`s notes.

Depreciation: Like inventory, choice of depreciation method also has drastic effects on financial statements both income statement and balance sheet). there are three elements related to depreciation are in management`s discretion.
- Schedule/method of depreciation
- Useful life of the asset.
- Salvage value of the asset.

Schedule/method of depreciation: we have
Straight line method: depreciation is spread equally on useful life of asset.
Accelerated method: Higher depreciation in early years of useful life of asset.
Usage based method: Higher allocation of depreciation in higher production season.
Useful life: higher the useful life management estimates, lower the depreciation expense.
Salvage value: Higher the salvage value estimates, lower the depreciation and vice versa.

We need to adjust depreciation expense so our understanding for the company`s depreciation expense improves and we would be able to compare it with other companies.

Unfortunately, from financial statements and disclosures we would not have enough information about asset and it`s depreciation. This is also because the assets are shown in aggregation and are in different of their useful life.

We can use some ratios to find some information about assets. For example, useful life of a company's asset = accumulated depreciation / gross property plant and equipment.

Number of years of depreciation expense that has been recognized so far = Accumulated depreciation /current depreciation expense. Useful life remaining on the overall asset = net property plant and equipment / depreciation expense. Average life of assets and installation = Gross property plant and equipment /depreciation expense.

There is another difference worth to mention. US GAAP does not allow upward valuation of fixed asset but it is permitted under IFRS. So, if a company reporting under IFRS and valuated an asset upward we need to reverse the upward valuation effect to compare it with a company operating under US GAAP.

Good will: Good will arises when a company acquires another company and pays more than fair value of the acquired assets. Good will goes into balance sheet as asset and is tested annually and written down if impaired.

There is problem of comparison between two companies with one has grown by acquisition and other has grown internally. The acquiring firm record good will by capitalizing the extra payment on acquisition while the internally grow company normally has expensed it`s growth expenditures. So how we compare them?

We can remove good will, other intangible assets (from balance sheet) and Impairment charges (from income statement). This will give us a better comparable view and ratios would make more sense must also be removed from income statement.

Off balance sheet financing: Capital lease (Finance lease) and its future payments are recorded in financial statements. Operation lease is not recorded but as we know it is an essential mode of financing and it must be considered while calculating ratios especially when comparing two companies one with capital while other with operating lease. We must calculate present value of future expected operating lease payments to get a better comparison with the firm using finance lease. Let's do it with the help of an example.

Following data is gives.

Year	Capital lease	Operating lease
2X12	$200000	$400000
2X13	$200000	$400000
2X14	$200000	$400000
2X15	$200000	$400000

Beyond 2X15	$800000	$900000

Present value of capital lease is $700000

To calculate present value, we need discount rate. For discount rate and other calculations, we have two methods.

1. **Assume the operating lease has the same ratio of present value to payments as firm`s capital lease.**

A total of $1600000 of capital lease and total of $2500000 of operating lease is to be paid in future.

Ratio of present value (of capital lease) to future payments = $\frac{700000}{1600000}$ =0.4573

Using this we can estimate PV of operating lease as,

PV of operating lease = 0.4573*2500000 =$1093750

2. **Estimate discount rate for capital lease and apply it to operating lease.**

To have a single discount rate for capital lease we have to have some assumptions like, we the capital lease to be fully paid in 6 or 7 years etc. if we assume total years of payment are 6 then we can find IRR which gives us PV equal to $700000. That IRR would be used for operating lease.

That's all for FRA. I wish best of luck to all students and I will be coming soon with more books

If you find this book helpful, would you be kind enough to leave a review for this book on Amazon? It will be highly appreciated. Click on following links.

For USA students
www.amazon.com/dp/B07G3288C9
For UK

www.amazon.co.uk/dp/B07G3288C9

For Indians
www.amazon.in/dp/B07G3288C9   ***Others   please   go   to   your***
appropriate Amazon